AF522240

Human Systems Management

DPH Management Series

Human Systems Management

J M DEWAN • K N SUDARSHAN

DISCOVERY PUBLISHING HOUSE
NEW DELHI-110002

Discovery Publishing House
4831/24, Ansari Road, Darya Ganj
New Delhi - 110 002 (INDIA)

Human Systems Management

ISBN-81-7141-362-5

PRINTED IN INDIA

Published by Discovery Publishing House, New Delhi and Lasertypeset at Technographics and Printed at Arora Offset Press, Delhi.

Preface

The management world is in transition. The causes of this transition are many, but the major one is the vast changes in knowledge and in the information that flows in and out of organizations. This changing information disrupts traditions, established processes, well-known procedures, and routine ways of doing things. New principles, concepts, techniques, ideas, expressions, processes, and procedures are emerging, moving us to a new plateau of professional practice. Trying to capture this changing knowledge and information is like trying to capture the atmosphere. How can you do it when the atmosphere is continually shifting and when you need the atmosphere to do the capturing? The best we can do is find a peak from which we can at least get a perspective on management as a whole, decide on the work and responsibilities of management, and gather in whatever practical management information we can. A team of experts in this series represent some of the best contemporary thinking and information available. They represent many major successful corporations, active consulting agencies, and well-known educational institutions, and all are experts on what is happening with the flow of knowledge and information in the management world. This is a lofty pinnacle from which to survey the management world.

Managers and supervisors clamor for current information and guidelines to help solve formidable problems in their work world—problems that range from "how to do it" to "how to resolve conflict when doing it." Many problems are generated from miscommunication and incompetence. As the management practice proceeds from the complex to the supercomplex, problem solving becomes a large-scale challenge requiring new knowledge and skills. Managers and supervisors cannot wait for research breakthroughs with real-world answers to solve these dilemmas. They must tackle them here and now with the useful information and proven practices immediately available. Whether making a decision, solving a problem setting up a procedure, designing a process, or resolving a behaviour conflict, a manager must rely heavily on information. To a great extent, management practitioners are information workers; that is, they generate, distribute, store, retrieve, and consume information. Competence in finding and using the right information at the needed time determines to a considerable extent competence in the management function, activity, or responsibility. The *DPH Management Series* attempts to fill this need for usable information in spite of the changing nature of its subject.

The *DPH Management Series* not a book to be read and later discarded. It is a reference book, a tool to be used by managerial personnel in the day-to-day work of an organization. Like a tool, it should never be more than a reach away when a new situation emerges that demands its use. This series aim to achieve a first-and practical and proven knowledge and information as a self-development opportunity for those who are moving into or upward in management. A complete spectrum of management subjects is immediately available for orientation, study, analysis, assimilation, and problem solving. Within one set of covers is the view of management as a totality. The management field is loaded with ideas that the organization of this handbook series unique logic. It follows both levels and areas of responsibilities of an organization.

The work of this handbook series is the collaborative effort of many outstanding people in the management field. The motivation for this work varied from individual to individual, but the central motivation that united us all was the excitement of capturing the management state-of-the-art and sharing it with colleagues in the dynamic profession of management.

This series should be of great help to managerial practitioners at any organizational level who are responsible for a function, department, or set of responsibilities. The handbook series will also give these practitioners insights into management roles and approaches in other areas as well. The subject matter encompasses top, middle, and lower management. Special emphasis was placed on managing people, time, space, budgets, and resources to give the handbook extra utility for middle and lower management. Students of management in university or educational institutions will find the series an invaluable resource for adding "real world" practices to their academic and theoretical foundations. MBA students will gain an invaluable overview of the total organization to complement their MBA degree. Administrators and public managers can become acquainted with practices employed by managers and supervisors in private organizations. These practices are not always directly applicable in public sector bodies, but with thought and modifications, these private practices can adapt to public organizations. Public and university librarians will find the handbook an indispensable reference for the multitude of questions on many topics from the general public, special groups, associations, and students.

Editors

Contents

1 Organizational Innovation: Competing Models of Productive Efficiency

Introduction

It is widely agreed, within a burgeoning international literature, that the world of production—factories, workshops, offices—is undergoing a profound transformation. Job structures and management processes which worked well in the past, involving tight task delineation and discipline, are now seen as fetters, restraining the flexibility and market responsiveness that firms need to survive. The talk now in management and production circles is of 'new production systems', or of an emergent spectrum of 'world best practices' in manufacturing and service delivery, or of a 'new workplace culture'. For the past decade debate has centred on the prospects for the mass production system, perfected in the USA but now under great stress there, while the Japanese challenge has been recognised and assimilated in what is called the 'lean production system', seen by many as a world-historic successor to mass production. A skills-based, human-centred alternative is also being discussed and promoted, variously called the anthropocentric production system, or 'high performance' work system, or 'sociotechnical' system, that turns out to provide a positive institutional framework for the introduction of advanced manufacturing systems and client-centred service systems in countries with strong democratic traditions.

These sharply diverging paradigms are intellectual constructs, but they reflect real divergences in production strategies, in work structures, in management styles, and most fundamentally, in the business strategies pursued by firms. There is no longer a 'one best way' to the perfection of production efficiency. A more complex world now demands a more complex approach to the design, negotiation and implementation of systems for the production of goods and of services.

In the current period of turbulence, as markets become global and more sophisticated, there is seemingly no end to the round of exhortations driving firms to improve their performance—by introducing 'new technology', or by adopting 'best practice'. The familiar battery of acronyms is summoned up as saviours: CAD-CAM, FMS, AMT, EFTPOS, EDI, TQM, JIT, and most comprehensive of all, CIM. Government programs offer strong incentives to firms which are prepared to install such systems. But there is by now abundant evidence that it is not these systems themselves that are responsible for improved performance. It is the way in which they are used, or more exactly, the way in which they mesh with the organisational business and strategies being pursued by the firm, which is of crucial importance. For example, it is not 'new technology' itself which rejuvenates a firm, but the way in which computer-based, programmable systems are used to enhance flexibility or, conversely, to intensify existing rigidities. Simple approaches to rationalisation and labour-shedding automation, or frank deskilling, might seem attractive to firms which see their competitive advantage lying in standardisation and reduced costs. Firms which see their future more in terms of enhanced quality, product differentiation and rapid response, will probably be interested in using programmable systems to extend the flexibility of their existing skills-based work systems.

These choices lie at the heart of the transformations which are currently being wrought in production systems. What confuses the issue is the intellectual baggage that firms bring with them from a time when things were simpler. The competing paradigms of production systems reflect contested views of what it is that constitutes productive efficiency. In turn, the choices of production system are connected with choices involving business strategy, i.e., with where the firm situates itself in the market.

One dominant view is still that efficiency is associated with the division of labour, with fragmentation of jobs, with the embodiment of routines in programs and automation that eliminate the 'uncertain' factor of human work from the production cycle—the old dream of the workerless factory. Such views have a rationality of their own that connects them with business strategies oriented towards volume production of standardised, commodified goods. As firms with such strategies have found themselves under increasing pressure from low-cost competitors in low-wage countries, increasingly they have been forced to look beyond such simple strategies. Thus market segments have arisen in which products have shorter life cycles, and are developed with shorter lead times; when products are more closely attuned to customer and market demands; when product variety, diversity and quality are the determinants of competitive success. Under these circumstances, it is firms which are prepared to adopt new production systems which gain a competitive edge. Such firms are prepared to experiment with non-authoritarian teamwork structures that dispense with traditional supervisory and surveillance systems; they are prepared to experiment with new programmable routines for switching products and services as market preferences change; they are prepared to enter into closer collaborative relations with both their customers and suppliers. They are prepared to utilise computer-based systems to enhance the decision-making powers of skilled, responsible workers, rather than seeking to eliminate them. They seek to achieve these heightened states of awareness through managed, negotiated processes of change, rather than through top-down, 'big bang' transformations.

This paper then will address three principal issues:

- What are the models of productive efficiency that underlie the term 'best practice'?
- What are the organisational structures that embody these models of productive efficiency?
- What are the effects of different industrial relations systems in facilitating or frustrating the transition to the new production systems?

These questions are investigated in the concrete setting of case studies of real organisational change in Australia. At the University of New South Wales I have been researching these issues in a series of studies that span manufacturing, processing industry and services, in both the public and private sectors.

It can be argued that Australia provides a kind of accelerated laboratory of organisational innovation—from the very retarded to the very advanced in a few short years. The country's industrial culture has changed within the past decade from a complacent, resources-driven economy with a small, protected and lazy manufacturing industry, to one which is driven by competitive, export-oriented value-adding activities that have called forth a revolution in the institutional framework of industry and industrial relations. In this context, the lineaments of a distinct 'Australian model' that draws on several elements of international experience, are emerging.

While it is difficult to draw general conclusions from such a small sample, nevertheless these studies point to an arresting between the emergence of new, collaborative forms of work and the new, cooperative industrial relations of organisational and technological change. A similar alignment lies at the heart of recent research findings from advanced industrial sectors in Europe, America and East Asia, to be discussed below.

Competing production systems

It is by now relatively uncontroversial to claim that a spectrum of new production systems is emerging in OECD countries, based on high quality, quick response and high value-added product strategies. These stand in contrast with the standardised low value-added production system, based on mass production, that has dominated the twentieth century until the most recent decade. The lineaments of the new production systems are by now reasonably familiar; they have been described by a number of recent authors, both individuals and institutions. Two dominant forms of new production system are emerging in advanced industrial countries. One is associated with the lean production system that emerged first in Japan; it is being introduced by many firms as a total system calling for comprehensive changes in manufacturing, sales, supply, with teams operating in subordination to total system requirements. It is called in this paper the 'lean production system'. The other is an indigenous team-based alternative, that seeks flexibility through the autonomy of self-managing teams that have some control over their own quality assurance, their logistics, maintenance and other associated activities. Team-based cellular manufacturing and team-based client-centred service delivery best exemplify this new production system, variously described as 'human-centred'. 'anthropocentric', or 'American teamwork'. In this paper, it is called the 'sociotechnical production system', since most of its distinctive features were actually identified by the sociotechnical school that emerged at London's Tavistock Institute in the 1960s.

The new production systems are no passing fad or 'flavour of the month'. They are here to stay. A number of factors are at work here, but we might mention just three.

First, the new production systems as innovations differ from previous management innovations such as matrix structures or 'management by objectives' in a fundamental way. Important as these initiatives may have been, they did not engaged directly with the way that work is productively performed. Rather than reforming the management of inefficient work procedures, the new production systems represent a reform of the work structures themselves. And by getting to the fundamentals of reorganising the way that work is performed, they bring in their wake an equally fundamental reform of the process of management itself. In place of command and control structures designed to enforce rigidity and compliance, the new production systems call for management that offers facilitation, guidance and coordination between self-managing groups of employees who are capable of looking after the details of production for themselves.

Second, the new production systems also differ sharply from the various job redesign and 'quality of working life' initiatives that were popular in workplaces in the 1970s—such as job rotation and job enlargement. Important as these initiatives may have been, they never got to grips with the fundamentals of why work was structured in such a fragmented way. The QWL initiatives grappled with the symptoms, but not with the cause of workplace inefficiencies. They never came to grips with the fundamentals of enhancing the responsibility carried by employees for achieving better results, which is the issue that underpins all the new production systems.

Third, the move to new production systems is concerned with the quality of the outputs of the production process, rather than being obsessed solely with the cost of the inputs. Traditional approaches to productivity improvement have almost always taken cost cutting as their driving feature. But if the outputs are not being improved-which is the goal of the new production systems-there is little scope for competitive advancement through cutting the costs of inputs, other than by sliding down to a cheaper level in the market place. And this is a slippery slope that most firms would want to avoid. While all firms need to budget and control their costs, the point is to what extent costs are allowed to determine business and production strategy.

The mass production system

There is by now a strong consensus that the 'traditional' forms of work being ousted by the new production systems, trace their origins to the mass production system. As an example of this new consensus, we may accept the arguments advanced by the MIT Commission on Industrial Productivity, in their hard-hitting 1989 book *Made in America*. The Commission's analysis was centred on the role of mass production in shaping the prevailing concepts of productivity and efficiency, and in determining the prevailing patterns of industrial relations. As the MIT Commission noted, 'The great success of the American economy in the twentieth century was a system of mass production of standard products for a large domestic market'. Competitive advantage lay with simple, low value-added products that could be produced at low cost in large numbers for undifferentiated mass markets.

A substantial literature now documents the origins, rise to dominance and loss of dominance of a production system based on standardised production. It has been extended to encompass the impact mass production techniques have had on management practices, in particular on accounting, as well as on culture more generally. In the recent work of Chandler it has been given a definitive comparative dimension, utilising the general categories of a 'competitive managerial capitalism' which arose in the US and a 'cooperative managerial capitalism' in Germany, both superseding the 'personal' or 'proprietorial' capitalism of 19th century Britain; managerial capitalism has in turn been succeeded as dominant system by the 'collective capitalism' of Japan and the Far East in the later 20th century.

This system was replicated, with varying national adjustments, in virtually all OECD countries during the post-war period. It called for narrow jobs and the pursuit of efficiency through division of labour, for detail work to be regulated by machine and by close, untrusting supervision; for skills to be appropriated by Organisation and Methods engineering departments, and to be confined to narrow 'trades' protected by demarcation and the 'front end' training model of apprenticeship. Deskilling was pursued as a conscious strategy, in order to cheapen labour and hence production; technological innovation was pursued to further deskill and eliminate the labour 'factor' in the production process.

The paradigm shift in manufacturing captured in the phrase 'new production concepts' owes its origins to market segmentation and innovation on the demand side, and to the development of new work organisation systems such as teamwork and programmable flexible manufacturing and assembly systems, on the supply side. In the realm of complex value-added goods and services, these organisational innovations have given firms adopting them a competitive edge over firms which are still wedded to large-scale mass production as their strategy.

So we have an analysis of mass production as

a system whose canons of productive efficiency are as shown in table.

The mass production system

Organisational features:

- Standardisation of product
  (competitive advantage based on price)
- Standardisation of process
  (moving assembly lines; long, stable production runs)
- Standardisation of labour
  (Taylorism, divorce of conception from execution)

Outcomes:

- Low quality, low cost products
- Functional division of labour
- High inventories and buffer stocks
- Labour rigidities and demarcations

Inputs:

- Low trust, arms length customer and supplier relations
- Centralised authority/hierarchies
- Low trust industrial relations

Taken together, these canons of efficiency have come to dominate the discourse of productivity in the 20th century. It is now taken as virtually self-evident, at least in the popular mind, that efficiency is synonymous with division of labour, with centralisation of expertise, with hierarchies of control—all features of the Mass Production System. Within the MPS proper they had a clear rationale—even if in practice they led to extreme social conflict and sometimes inhuman working conditions, particularly where Taylorisation was combined with rationalisation of jobs in large bureaucracies. But outside the MPS, which after all never attained a majority proportion of productive activity in any country, not even the USA-outside this system, these canons of efficiency had no purchase at all. Yet they have achieved almost total dominance of our views as to what constitutes efficiency, being seen to apply to batch-based production work and even to the activities of public sector agencies such as transport and health systems that have nothing in common with the MPS. This is one of the striking paradoxes of the 20th century.

Our understanding of current best practice in workplace reform and organisational innovation, starts with an appreciation of the limits to the mass production systems, and hence of the reach and applicability of its canons of productive efficiency. The next step in the argument is to consider the real alternatives that have arisen to mass production. This means looking beyond the superficial innovations mentioned above such as matrix management and QWL initiatives—for these did not engage with the logic of mass production. They merely sought to soften its effects. But genuine alternatives have arisen, which is one of the reasons that the mass production paradigm is now under such strain.

The lean production system

Historically, the first comprehensive alternative to the mass production system emerged in Japan. Evolving out of a replication of US mass production systems, the Toyota production system in particular was already in the 1950s developing a markedly different model of productive efficiency. The reasons for this are now coming to be understood—after a lengthy period of miscomprehension that veiled Japanese developments behind an inscrutable cultural barrier.

For a start, the Japanese market was much smaller than the US, and so extreme dependence on long runs of identical products was never seen as an option. Secondly, Toyota early on conceived its comparative advantage over US and European mass producers in terms of the skills of its work-force - so it never sought the extremes of deskilling that were pursued in North America. Building on these skills, it strove for continuous, incremental improvement in its production processes, ignoring the Taylorist injunction to seek and stick with the 'one best way'. The reliance on skills also led in a natural progression to an emphasis on building quality into production work. Out of this flowed the notion of reducing inventories, which were needed in other plants as a buffer between poor production and disrupted supply. Thus was born the Just-In-Time approach, which in retrospect can be seen as a powerful joint learning technique involving collaboration between a producer and its components suppliers.

While none of these elements on its own could be said to mark a decisive break with the technoeconomic base of mass production, together they amounted to a rupture with the model of productive efficiency associated with Frederick

Winslow Taylor and rigorously adhered to in the west at the time that Toyota was developing its alternative. The system developed by Toyota has since been picked up by other Japanese manufacturers, in the automotive industry and beyond. This is the system that is now called the Lean Production System.

The lean production system is seen as a total system that encompasses fundamentally new approached to running the factory; to design new products; to coordinating the supply chain; to linking customers with other aspects of the business; and finally to the management of the total enterprise, as summarised in table.

The MIT group argue that Lean Production is an integrated system that will become the dominant paradigm in the 21st century. They argue that these paradigm shifts take decades to accomplish; for example, it took 50 years for mass production to diffuse from the US to Europe and Asia. The LPS has taken the best part of three decades to develop in Japan; it started to spread quickly to the US and Europe in the 1980s, and will become, they say, a global force in the 1990s.

The lean production system

Organisational features:

- Diversified mass production
  (competitive advantage based on price, quality and responsiveness)
- Flexibility of process
  (quick change-over; just-in-time)

- Functional flexibility of labour (multi-tasking)

Outcomes:

- High quality, low cost products
- Functional integration of labour
- Low inventories and no buffer stocks
- Labour flexibility, continuous improvement

Inputs:

- High commitment, close customer and supplier relations
- Team-based hierarchies
- Medium-trust industrial relations
- High worker commitment to company

The best indicator so far of the success of the LPS outside Japan, is in the so-called Japanese transplants, such as the automotive companies run by Toyota, Honda, Mazda and others in overseas countries. The Japanese 'transplants' have now been studied and their output measured. Krafcik found that Japanese automobile plants in the US required on average 19.6 hours to produce a vehicle, compared with 20.3 hours in Japan, and 24.4 hours in average US plants. This is the material effect of a lean production system. In other words, the transplants have achieved a level of efficiency comparable to that obtained in their home base. Efforts are now being made by automotive manufacturers to go beyond 'transplants', and embody some of the LPS principles in their own operations. A group of European manufacturers have formed the European Automobile Initiative Group to promote such initiatives.

But it is likely that the real significance of

lean production will be felt beyond the automotive industry, in manufacturing more generally, and more broadly in the services sector, as firms find their 'mass production' approaches becoming counter-productive. Now LPS principles are being extended into general manufacturing by such agencies as engineering consultancy firms.

Limits to the LPS

As a system, the LPS has successfully overturned the Taylorist canons of productive efficiency erected by the MPS in firms seeking diversity and quality of output. But in their place it has established a new and potentially dangerous orthodoxy, namely that the system is more important than its component parts. In the tightly integrated lean production system, operating on razorsharp just-in-time principles, the least variation leads to seizure of the production apparatus. Apart from the contribution that people make to improvements via Quality Circles and other forms of involvement, the contributions that they make on the job are tightly constrained.

It is these systemic constraints that are widely seen, both within Japan and externally, as constituting the limits to expansion of the LPS.

In Japanese LPS companies, workers on assembly lines still perform short-cycle repetitive operations that can be executed in less than one minute. In such cases, the LPS can only be described as a modified form of Taylorism. Critics of the LPS outside Japan, such as Berggren point to these features as being of the essence of LPS, and hence as drastically opposed to Western traditions of job redesign in its most participative mode. European alternatives such as Volvo, with its team-based assembly systems using alternatives to the traditional assembly line, at Kalmar and most recently at Uddevalla, have long seen as constituting the case against the endless expansion of production facilities based on LPS principles.

Of even greater significance, the LPS is under exacting scrutiny in Japan. It is now recognised by many parties in Japan, including the Ministry of International Trade and Industry, that the JIT system carries heavy social costs as small transport vehicles making hourly deliveries clog the roads. The system of externalising costs through subcontracting is also coming under scrutiny, and pressure applied to final assemblers to take on more of the costs themselves. Mazda, for example, is now making efforts to internalise many of the social costs imposed by the LPS.

Critics in Japan point to the alienating features of work organised along strictly LPS lines outside the automotive industry. Nomura for example took the case of automated assembly work in an electronics factory, where printed circuit boards were being fabricated for television sets. Masami Nomura, from Okayama University, and colleagues, argued that the approach to productivity enhancement in this factory followed traditional rationalisation and automation lines, with automation seeking to eliminate jobs, and the workforce being divided into a 'core' and periphery that followed gender divisions. High productivity was maintained by long working hours. The conclusion was that 'The division of labor in Japan is a kind of Taylorism which will hardly be maintained under pressure from abroad.

If this is the case, what kind of alternative can be constructed as a genuine successor and competitor to both the MPS and LPS?

Sociotechnical production system

A quite different intellectual tradition is involved in the generation of the third alternative production system paradigm. This is the tradition that derives from 'human relations' insights, which all through the 20th century have been at odds with Taylorism. This paradigm is fundamentally concerned with the role of people at the centre of the production process. It has variously been called human-centred, anthropocentric, sociotechnical, or 'high performance' work system, and it traces its lineage through the semi-autonomous work groups and industrial democracy experiments associated with the Tavistock Institute, back to human relations organisational theorists such as Douglas McGregor and Kurt Lewin.

In honour of these intellectual antecedents, I propose that this model be termed the Sociotechnical Production System.

The point about the STPS is not its name, but its applicability to the moving front of organisational innovation in both manufacturing and services. The clearest expression of the STPS is team-based cellular production systems, appearing in various manufacturing, processing and services sectors, where the team members carry authority and responsibility for achieving production targets, for ensuring quality standards, and for following through all the scheduling and coordination issues involved in meeting these targets. Computer systems and other forms of information technology are used in such systems as extensions of the skills already acquired and used collaboratively by cell members. Numerous examples of such production systems have been described in the literature. The cases that I have observed myself are described in the UNSW studies.

While various aspects of the STPS have been analysed in the management, manufacturing and services literatures, I wish to emphasise the common model that informs all of these developments, and above all the constitutional legitimation of such systems through a framework of industrial relations founded on what Kochan and Dyer call 'mutual commitment'.

Like its predecessor, the human relations school, the STPS provides both a positive model of new production systems, and a critique of dominant practices, reminding the parties to industrial negotiations that the human element must always be central to production. As in its terminology, it calls for a balance between the social and technical dimensions of the change process.

The point of calling this a system alternative to LPS is that it incorporates all the insights of the LPS regarding the elimination of wasteful activities—but it does so with a firm understanding that ultimately people constitute the source of productivity improvement. In the STPS, machines are devised to extend the capacities of productive people-rather than in the MPS, people being seen as mere extensions of a machine, or as in the LPS, people frequently being sacrificed to the systemic coordination that is the hallmark of the LPS efficiency.

There are a number of intellectual sources for the STPS. We may identify at least four streams of thought and experience:

- human relations;
- sociotechnical systems;
- new production concepts;
- human-centred systems.

Let us look briefly at each, before considering how they fit into current episodes of restructuring associated with the advent of Information Technology, such as intelligent manufacturing and business process re-engineering.

Human relations school

The human relations school has existed as a source of critique of Taylorism ever since the 1920s and 30s, when it was becoming clear that firms organising their production systems by the rigorous application of Taylor's methods, could not hope to sustain their competitive advantages. While conventional organisational behaviour theory traces the origins of human relations thinking to Mayo and the Hawthorne experiments conducted at Western General Electric, it is more fruitful to base the arguments on the work of Kurt Lewin and his practical demonstrations of the contribution made by teamwork and the effect of different leadership styles on the work of teams. Through original notions such as 'group dynamics', he was able to strike a blow at the very foundations of mechanistic notions of productive efficiency.

The human relations school eventually became subsumed within the Organisational Development school in the US, which in its insistence on participation without leadership, and its studied ignoring of industrial relations, has largely departed from the realistic assumptions of human relations, and is not counted here as a source for the STPS. This stream terminated in the ideas of job enrichment and job enlargement propagated by such authors as Herzberg, and which came together in the broad notion of Quality of Working Life improvements. In retrospect, this can be seen as an evolutionary dead-end that had little practical impact on workplace reform and innovation.

Sociotechnical school

In contrast to the purely social insights of the human relations school, and to the purely technical innovations of Taylorist-inspired engineers, a new school of thought emerged in the 1950s insisting that successful change would have to accommodate both social and technical features of change. It was through their insistence on this point, that researchers at the Tavistock Institute, London, came to be known as the 'socio-technical' school. Their ideas have since been exported around the world.

While there have been many alternatives propose to Taylorism and work bureaucratisation, the sociotechnical approach was the first to be promoted systematically and successfully as a practical alternative to the prevailing paradigm. It was in fact promoted explicitly, by exponents such as Trist and Emery, as 'the emergence of a new paradigm of work'. Nothing that has happened since has invalidated this view. The more recent arrival of information technology innovation has merely underscored the basic soundness of the original sociotechnical insights.

The Tavistock Institute of Human Relations had been founded as a novel, interdisciplinary, action-oriented research organisation in 1946 with the aid of a grant from the Rockefeller Foundation. It was set op for the specific purpose of actively relating the psychological and social sciences to broad social concerns. Pioneering studies had been conducted of the social system of factory work, published as the celebrated Glacier study, but as yet the action-oriented researchers had not formulated a specific link with technology, and so were unable to propose a work system as an alternative to the mass production model.

In 1950 as part of a government-funded research programme investigating organisational innovations that could raise productivity in industry, Eric Trist and his group 'discovered 'the existence of self-regulating groups in underground coal mines, leading to the formulation of the notion of the 'semi-autonomous work group' which has been central to socio-technical theory ever since.

The Tavistock researchers went on to generalise this coalmining discovery, and the principles of joint-optimisation of the social and technical systems of work soon became well established as alternatives to the prevailing Taylorist approach and to the human relation approach. As Trist put the matter, in his 1981 overwiew of the entire sociotechnical experience, this joint approach could be enunciated in the form of seven principles:

1) The work system, which comprised a set of activities that made up a functioning whole, now became the basic unit rather than the single jobs into which it was decomposable.

2) Correspondingly, the work group became central, rather than the individual job-holder.

3) Internal regulation of the system by the group was thus rendered possible rather than the external regulation of individuals by supervisors.

4) A design principles based on the redundancy of functions rather than the redundancy of parts, introduced by Emery, characterised the

underlying organisational philosophy which tended to develop multiple skills in the individual and immensely increase the response repertoire of the group.

5) This principle values the discretionary rather than the prescribed part of work roles.

6) It treated the individual as complementary to the machine rather than as an extension of it.

7) It was variety-increasing for both the individual and the organisation rather than variety decreasing in the bureaucratic mode.

The parallel stream of thought that had been developed in the form of the 'human relations' school, whose practical proposals were picked up as job enrichment and jobs enlargement - was opposed vehemently by sociotechnical theorists as being too weak. These disputes have lost their fire today, when we can see that both schools were opposing Taylorism, and neither were at that time making much headway against the logic of mass production.

The sociotechnical school obtained its first substantial application in the form of a series of innovations in Norwegian industry, conducted with Einar Thorsrud, and known as the Norwegian 'Industrial Democracy' programme. These innovations spread to Sweden, where they were taken up with rather greater gusto, as in the famous examples of Volvo work reorganisation experiments at Kalmar. There experiences have been taken up and generalised by a group of researchers at the Stockholm Centre for Working Life, led by Bjorn Gustavsen.

Parallel to the Anglo-American developments that grew out of socio-technical systems, there emerged a German industrial psychological approach termed Action Regulation Theory. Like socio-technical systems, it was concern with the design of jobs and the formulation of criteria defining 'good' jobs.

Then one glaring 'absence' in the classical socio-technical tradition, as in the German Action Regulation Theory, was recognition of the arrival of a quite different alternative in Japan, in the form of the lean production system, and the implications that this would carry for job design in Europe. The Tavistock research were apparently unaware of what was happening at Toyota while they were investigating the emergence of teamwork in western countries. This is why in our exposition today we have to recognise three dominant paradigms, or models, of productive efficiency, rather than the dichotomy propounded by the sociotechnical school in its formative writings.

New production concepts in europe

In Europe, partly in response to the Japanese challenge and partly in response to new competitive pressures and demands from trade unions for humanisation of work, observers were noting important shifts in organisation in the early 1980s. Industrial sociologists Kern and Schumann conducted a survey in core sectors of the German economy, in machine tools, automobiles and chemicals, and announced their discovery of 'new production concepts', meaning a form of organisation that broke with Taylorism. In follow-up surveys they have confirmed their previous findings, extending their analysis to the electronics industry.

These conceptual innovations have been amply confirmed in empirical investigations. For example, work by Christel Lane has shown that German industry has taken up these concepts whereas French and British industry has been slower to do so because of the prevailing attachment to notions of large-scale activity, centralisation and rationalisation as supposed sources of competitive strength.

Human-centred production system

A European alternative to both mass production and lean production, has been developed in the notion of human-centred production. This has now come to be called the Anthropocentric Production System. It is promoted in Europe, such as by the European Commission, as a genuine alternative to both the MPS and LPS.

The notion of human—centredness in production systems stems from formulations first advanced by Howard Rosenbrock and by Mike Cooley in the UK.

Both Rosenbrock and Cooley argued that the trend towards the 'unmanned factory', driven by distrust in the human operators and a desire to automate the human element 'out of the control loop', was fundamentally misconceived. They knew from their practical experience that adjustments always have to be made to automatic settings depending on a range of circumstances; this was a negative criterion for maintaining the input of skilled operators. More positively, such operators represented a unique source of creativity, flexibility and innovativeness—but their contribution could be accommodated only by designing systems around their involvement. Hence the notion of 'human-centredness', or treating the skilled operator as central, and the technology as an extension of the operator's capabilities, complementing his or her skills rather than displacing them.

Human-centred CIM

The ideas of the STPS has received a new lease of life with the advent of a programmable automation, leading to the concept of cellular manufacturing, or more generally, to human-centred cellular production. The criteria of human-centredness in the context of the latest manufacturing technology are being refined in a series of studies carried out in Europe under the Esprit programme of the European Commission.

Two demonstration production cells were established, at Rolls Royce in London, and at BICC Sealectro. The latter project involved the production of radio frequency connectors, using CNC equipments for turning, milling, heat treatment and assembly. The final report on the BICC cell conducts a preliminary investigation of the cost advantage of building the technology around the operators, which shows positive results, but the real value of these projects lies in their acting as test beds and feasibility demonstrations. As such they give rise to a new problematic of the 'social shaping of technology'.

The human-centred approach is starting to penetrate the literature on ergonomics and engineering design,in recognition of the fact that the notion of 'human-centredness' has to be refined into specific criteria governing the design process in a number of different contexts.

The most striking feature to have emerged from these experiments so far, is not so much the development of a set of criteria for human-centredness, but a recognition that human-centred production systems have to be organized in semi-autonomous or quasi self- sufficient cells. This is a powerful insight that links human-centredness to the developments in Cellular Manufacturing, which themselves have received a big fillip with the advent of CIM. Thus the circle closes, with the latest CIM cells making connection with the original notion of the 'semi-autonomous work group' introduced by sociotechnical researchers in the 1960s.

Dutch sociotechnical school

The most sophisticated current application of sociotechnical methods and principles to organisational renewal is the approach termed Integral Organisational Renewal. Because it was developed by a group of researchers in The Netherlands, it is now known as the Dutch sociotechnical school.

The essential characteristic of the Dutch approach is that is takes the entire organisation as its point of reference, embedding the production system in the organisational constellation that also includes new product development, joint action with suppliers, logistics, relations with customers, and other facets of the innovative and integrated organisation. This is a point of view that we shall come across repeatedly in our discussions: it is a view of the enterprise as a total system, as opposed to the various partial approaches to production reform that ignore, say, new product development, or approaches to marketing that ignore manufacture and design.

Competing models of productive efficiency

The abstract notions of 'production systems' exhibited here are not meant to represent world-historical ideas that march in some Hegelian order through history. They are meant, much more modestly, to capture the essential characteristics of the production decisions that individual firms make as they pursue their contrasting production strategies.

A firm which seeks to enhance its performance by further streamlining and rationalising tasks, by seeking further vertical integration operations, by introducing computer systems to automate processes that are presently performed by skilled staff-such a firmis actually deploying a model of productive efficiency that we can call a 'mass production model'. It makes sense if the firm is a mass producer in a world where competitive success goes to those firms which can secure economies of scale and scope through giant structures, and can service mass markets with products which sell on the basis of low price. But if the world does not reward such a competitive strategy, then the model of productive efficiency that is derived from it, is misplaced.

A firm which seeks to enhance its performance by linking tasks closely together, producing 'just in time' rather than 'just in case', by developing responsibilities and authority to shopfloor teams, by building quality assurance into jobs, and by building a production system as a comprehensive technology—such a firm is deploying a model of productive efficiency that we can call a 'lean production model'. It makes sense if the firm is seeking to compete in a rapidly changing market where success goes to speed of innovation, market responsiveness and quality of product rather than low price. It calls for high levels of worker commitment and input.

It is in providing the circumstances where such high levels of commitment may be anticipated, and a consensus in favour of innovation established, that the sociotechnical production system acquires its significance. In countries with a strong democratic tradition, such commitment cannot be assumed; rather it has to be created, through appropriate institutional frameworks such as industrial relations systems. But once created, the flexibility and autonomy of self-managing teams, operating within a context where change has a constitutional legitimacy through being negotiated collectively, provide firms with a powerful competitive advantage. Change that is agreed and self-managed, can be implemented quickly and thoroughly. This is increasingly the experience of firms introducing 'high performance' work systems in several countries.

The sociotechnical production system is applicable where a firm seeks to enhance its performance by seeking responsiveness through skilled and committed staff, working with tools and systems that extend their skills rather than displacing them, and where wasted activity is tackled through joint continuous improvement. It is grounded in what Walton and Kochan and Dyer call 'mutual commitment. Such a firm will seek out networks of customers and suppliers, and it will structure its own internal operations as a network of 'factories within a factory' or as customer-centred cells. The essence of its approach will be to seek technologies and work systems that build on and extend the skills of its employees.

The decision that firms make are concrete decisions taken in definite circumstances that never repeat themselves. To paraphrase the Greek philosophers, firms never step in the same market twice. But there are patterns discernible in the decisions that firms make, and this is what I am getting at in this notion of competing models of productive efficiency.

There has been criticism of the notion of competing 'models' or' paradigms' of management decision-making and work organisation. This criticism has been directed at similar two fold or three-fold categorisations, such as the one deployed in this paper. Much of this criticism has been directed at questions of historical accuracy in pin-pointing the time of appearance of the mass production system or the lean production system;such points are irrelevant when it is understood that the competing paradigms are co-existing and competing, rather than rolling through history like Hegelian world orders. A more substantial criticism has to do with the salience of capturing a complex set of inter-related organisational and business strategy issues within a set of two or three competing paradigms. But this is precisely the point of the exercise; it is precisely and attempt to lend coherence and order to organisational and business strategies that would otherwise be seen to be chaotic. This is the function of science.

In practice, the really significant question is whether the STPS, with its bias towards skilled operators, can prove to be a viable competitor with firms which embrace the LPS, with its bias towards a modified Taylorism. The evidence indicates it can be, and is, subject to a very important caveat.

It needs to be acknowledged the the scope of classical sociotechnical organisational design was, by today's standards, remarkably limited. The technical system was conceived as machinery and its spatiotemporal layout. The social system was deemed to comprise work or occupational roles in the production system proper; it virtually never sought to include technological design, new product development, marketing, accounting, nor any other of the numerous inter-related functions that make for successful enterprise. Indeed it is the strength of the Japanese lean production system that it does bring all these elements together into a coherent image to model of the successful enterprise.

This emphasis purely on production[7], at the expense of new product devlopment cost accounting and other necessary aspects of successful enterprise, is perhaps the most glaring weakness historically of sociotechnical theory. And it has cost companies dear. Volve, for example, perhaps the pre-eminent example in Europe of a company which has systematically sought to apply sociotechnical ideas in its car production divisions, has recently slipped badly and in 1992 announced that it would close its two 'flagship' plants at Kalmar and at Uddevalla. This meant that Volvo would henceforth be virtually indistinguishable from the other 'mass production' European vehicle producers, employing standard assembly line production techniques in a bid to stay abreast of Japanese competition. Berggren argues persuasively that Volvo has abandoned its sociotechnical experiments without giving them a real chance and that its real failure lay in the confinement of job redesign to factory production while new product development continued untouched in its exclusively engineering-based, sequential manner. In this it is very different from the systematic integration that takes place between production, marketing and supplies in Japanese new product development.

The same ideas apply, with even greater force, to the design of manufacturing systems and the criteria used by engineers. No-one should underestimate the need of the engineering profession for such 'metaguides to design, by which I mean criteria that stand outside of the design process but can inform it and engage with it. The depths to which such'uninformed' design can sink arc revealed in the relentless tendency to standardise manufacturing systems, reserving only the most mindless tasks for 'manual operations', and aiming to eliminate the 'human element' if at all possible. That this is still the typical approach was brought out in an important study conducted at Boston University, which surveyed the treatment of the 'human machine' interface in current, standard engineering textbooks. This study revealed a shocking absence of even the most elementary consideration regarding human skill or creativity; textbooks uniformly equated the 'human factor' with sources of uncertainty and under-performance, and established the engineering goal as one of eliminating human factors as their top priority.

Hence the salience to such engineers of a 'human centred' design paradigm, to jolt thinking on to new and potentially more fruitful lines. This has happened in the familiar manufacturing case if CIM. It is striking how it is now starting to make its appearance in 'human-centred' software engineering design, and even in human-centred design of flight deck control systems in Boeing aircraft. In this way the concept of human-centredness, as a metaguide for engineering design, is diffusing; the engine that drives this process is the competitive advantage reaped by firms which can describe their systems as being more flexible and more resilient precisely because they are 'human-centred'.

It is of course the market place that ultimately acts as the arbiter between competing paradigms. The competition between firms espousing different models of productive efficiency is intense. So the challenge for European industry, and for firms such as those in Australia which seek to compete on equal terms with Japanese firms deploying the LPS, is to rise above their traditional narrow conceptions of production, and harness all the resources at their disposal—which means forming a 'production coalition' with their skilled workforce in order to achieve substantially higher levels of productivity and efficiency. The institutional frameworks within which such coalitions are favoured, and within which they are curtailed, are thus of critical significance. This in turn brings the focus on issues of organisational change, and of industrial relations. In the final section of this paper, we shall outline three approaches to organisational transition and industrial relations, which embody and exemplify the three ideal types of the MPS, LPS and STPS.

Three worlds of industrial relations

In order to focus a discussion of the effects of

industrial relations framework, we may refer for convenience to the industrial relations of the mass production system, to the industrial relations of the lean production system, and in the case of best practice, to the industrial relations of the sociotechnical production system.

Let us establish the comparisons, to make these abstractions more precise.

Industrial relations of the mass production system

The canonical principles governing industrial relations in the MPS, start with the standardisation of labour, i.e. with Taylorist work organisation systems that break jobs down into meaningless fragments calling for task coordination to be provided through professional groups and supervisory hierarchies. Thus the classic ingredients of a MPS industrial relations collective bargaining agreement,are:

- narrow and numerous job classifications, based on machines rather than skills;
- wages geared to individual performance and job classifications;
- standardisation and specification of conditions of employment,with anomalies to be processed through complex grievance procedures;
- concentration of skills formation in the once-off'front-end' training programmes such as apprenticeship, and defence of such skills through strong union demarcations;
- limitation of the sphere of collective

bargaining, with union interventions limited to disputes resolution and grievance procedures.

This 'ideal type' of the MPS industrial relations is given its clearest expression in US collective bargaining contracts, but it is also expressed in Australian 'awards' handed down to cover entire industries by the industrial relations tribunals. We can see how such a system was functional within the MPS: It established stable and rigid demarcations and procedures, and institutionalised the exclusion of labour from production decision-making. But the question that immediately arises, is how efficient it might be in the context of changing production systems, when rigidity, standardisation and worker exclusion might not be so advantageous. The answer is clear: it is not efficient: indeed, it is a stumbling block to superior performance.

Industrial relations of the lean production system

The emergence of the LPS as a more flexible and innovative rival of the MPS brought with it a characteristic set of industrial relation arrangements, perfected first in Japan and still dominant in that country, where they have been institutionalised and become part of the national economy. The essential features of IR under the LPS, are:

- broad, skill-based job classifications;
- enterprise unions;
- seniority wages system;
- career paths for workers

- workers involvement via EI groups, QC circles etc.
- employment security guarantees.

As Koike has subtly observed, this IR system is essentially an extension to blue-collar factory workers of the conditions applying traditionally to white-collar workers; it represents the 'professionalisation' of workers. Along with the superior recognition and promotion of skills, the employment security guarantees and the seniority wages system, there was created an important elements of commitment to the enterprises that underwrites all the improvements in quality, productivity and product and process innovation that are the characteristic strength of the LPS. It is this commitment that underlies and transforms the apparent rigidities of the system, according to Dore.

Industrial relations of the sociotechnical production system

Against the background of a widespread shift in production strategies undertaken by firms in the US, Europe and Australia, major efforts have also been expended to broaden the narrow agenda of industrial relations, to encompass skills, work organisation, technology and culture, and to build trust and commitment into the system through institutionalising positive sum outcomes.

The ideal form that the emerging IR system has taken in these innovative firms and sectors, is along the following lines:

- broad job classification linked to levels of skill rather than to machines to technology;
- skills formation made a central feature of negotiated arrangements, e.g. creation of career paths, skills acquisition, time off for training etc.;
- work organisation arrangements made a feature of negotiated outcomes, such as explicit processes for forming and operating teams;
- wages based on skills acquired, as well as on group performance;
- participatives structures used to complement and enhance the levels of responsibility built into new job structures;
- single bargaining units at enterprise level, and enterprise-specific agreements;
- national and sectoral standards providing a framework within which enterprises reach their own agreements on the above elements.

All these elements can be found in best practice case studies. For example these arrangements offer obvious benefits, such as an end to alienating and degrading labour and a sense of involvement, commitment and responsibility. It spells the end to the 'psychosis of labour' that threatened workers in the meaningless jobs of the mass production system. For employers, the benefits are also substantial—in terms of functional flexibility, enhanced rates of product and process innovation, higher levels of quality assurance, and the improvements in measured performance criteria.

This is an industrial relations structure oriented towards innovation, responsiveness and flexibility, through eliminating the previous impediments, and providing enterprise-level flexibility within a framework laid down at the national to sectoral level. It also encourages the trust and commitment needed to secure high performed production, by making both parties to the agreement dependent on its successful operation for their rewards. This is the cybernetic, 'feed back' feature of STPS-enterprise agreements that is one of their most dynamic features. The agreement is predicated on its being implemented successfully, so both sides have an interest in ensuring that it is implemented in the way envisaged.

It is worth commenting on the strong enterprise focus of the STPSM IR framework. The above characterisation brings to the fore the enterprise character of many of the categories involved in skills formation, job design and technological change.

While sector level and national negotiations can set overall standards and qualifications, the details still need to be worked out at enterprise level. This focus on the industrial relations of the STPS thus provides us with an unexpected but plausible explanation for the current trend in industrial relations towards enterprises bargaining. Most discussions of this matter take the 'rigidities' of the industrial relations system as their starting point, and pose enterprise bargaining as a flexible solution to these rigidities.

This is what might be called the 'endogenous' explanation, locating the impetus towards enterprise negotiation within the present industrial relations system.

By contrast, the perspective I am developing is 'exogenous', in that it locates the impetus towards an enterprise focus in the changes that are occurring in the production system, with shifts in industrial relations reflecting and registering these changes. This is perhaps the critical feature of industrial relations systems in shaping enterprise security and enhanced performance.

This chapter has attempted to demonstrate that there is a logic, or pattern, to the decisions made by firms as they struggle for competitive advantage in conditions of turbulence. The logic makes itself felt in the coherence that flows from a business decision to focus, for example, on repetitive, standardised production, and the need for rigidity that this entails, as contrasted with the need for flexibility and autonomous decision-making that a different kind of business decision, favouring innovation and market responsiveness, entails.

Of course the real world of industry and commerce is never as tidy as the models or constructs introduced by scientific observers. There will indeed be few examples of 'pure' production systems introduced along the MPS, LPS or STPS lines, with their associated industrial relations and organizational change strategies. In practice, firms are groping for what appears to be workable at any time, and their strategies will inevitably draw something from all three models. But the greater coherence a firm can generate, the greater its chances of success.

What is clear is that there is no single model of 'best practice' emerging to take the place of Taylor's 'one best way' that he saw as the goal of scientific management. The more I study these issues, the more I am struck by the diversity of forms emerging as the rigidities of the mass production model are dispensed with. The implication is that there is space for creative interventions at the level of the enterprise, for managers and for workers and their unions, and at the level of public policy. Choices are inescapable. My argument is that the character of these choices will have far-reaching implications for firms themselves, as well as wider social and economic effects. These choices will determine the wealth of nations in the coming decade.

2 Competitiveness as Hyper-Strategy

Introduction

Achieving competitiveness has become a mission, or mantra for many of today's corporations and nations. Yet 'competitiveness' is rarely defined in ways that carry coherent strategic implications. One difficulty, or ambiguity, concerns the distinction between competitiveness conceived of as winning, or beating-the-opposition, versus competitiveness-as-success, or realisation-of-potential. Another definitional problem arises when one considers the diversity of types of strategic-entity, made possible by technological change. Thus, when formulating competitive strategy. It has become increasingly necessary to ask who or what is intended to win and who is to be beaten, which entities are to succeed and which are to fail?

This chapter explores these ambiguities and provides an answer to these questions. Following a discussion of competitiveness concepts and strategic-entities the conceptual framework of 'Strategy-as-Rationality' is briefly described, then used to express the twinned ambiguities of competition and entity within the general theory of rationality. As with other strategic mysteries changing notions of competitiveness can be informed by developments within the general theory. Specifically, the emerging concept of synergies amongst the distinctive forms of rationality, within any strategic entity, now enables a re-formulation of competitiveness. The approach is primarily attributable to Ritzer and Le Moyne but it also has other roots in theory and practice, spread out quite widely. In subsequent sections of the paper, new methodologies of strategy formulation and strategic analysis are considered, together with necessary adaptations and transitions.

Competitiveness

In the last decade or so, there has been increasing acceptance of the need to re-think traditional paradigms of economic competition and business competitiveness in strategic management. In the major contribution to strategic management from Economic theory, most notable in the work of M. Porter the term 'competitiveness' has mostly been used to mean:

- The degree of cost-leadership of a firm, combined with the level of differentiation, or perceived quality, of its outputs.
- The level of rivalry in an industry as determined by the strength of the five 'forces', such as the threat of new entrants.

- The combined strength of several inter-related economic and industry factors that influence the viability of an industry in a global economy.

With these concepts in mind, popular methodologies of competitive strategic analysis, have characterised the competitive strategy of corporations as a form of conflict between warrior-like entities, complete with competitive weapons, terms of engagement and battles. These methodologies, in turn, have reinforced an ideology and Zeitgeist within which making wealth is just like making war. As a result, a marked distinction is drawn between friend, in-group, the company, or us, versus the enemy, an outgroup, the competition, or them. Indeed, consultants purveying such competitive analysis techniques have urged their clients to become obsessed with winning battles. Such 'obsession' is surely ironic when one considers the central place occupied by forms of rationality in all Economic theories.

To win or succeed?

It is more than a decade since K. Boulding described the warlike notion of competitiveness-as-winning as 'a gross misunderstanding of the complexities of the system'. Thus, a complementary perspective now also sees any given strategic-entity as 'competing' primarily against itself, or an imagined ideal version, or vision of itself. The entity is seen to be engaged in a battle to fully realise its own potential so that 'achieving competitiveness' is taken to mean overcoming limitations, rather than necessarily outwitting, beating or defeating others.

With this perspective, the emphasis in strategy formulation shifts towards the development of human and technological capabilities, or learning. In addition, it becomes more directly apparent that the success of any strategic entity depends upon the 'success of other entities, rather than their defeat, or domination. Put differently, one wins with others, not against them. There is no need to rely upon elaborate metaphor and simulation to see much evidence of this. Several empirical studies of firms, nations and regions have each reported the success of entities whose strategies emphasise learning, cooperation and consensus. In each case these have been contrasted with less successful or less 'competitive' strategies that have imposed hierarchical control or more directly sought market dominance.

Ambiguities

The contrast between competitiveness-as-winning versus competitiveness-as-success becomes most salient when one views knowledge-systems as strategic entities, with knowledge as a form of capital. Such systems co-evolve, learn and share various types of information and know-how. With this interpretation, the ambiguous meaning of competitiveness is seen to be directly linked to another important ambiguity, concerning the nature, scope and boundary of multiple types of 'competitive' strategic entity. Accordingly, it is no coincidence that researchers and scholars in many fields have recently asked the question : 'who or what is.....

Deciding, in theories of decision making.

Trusting whom, in the international area.

Being rational, economic and other models.

Being moral, in ethical theory and business ethics.

and, especially, who or what is competing with and cooperating with whom',. In sum, it has now become necessary to attempt to formulate competitive strategy with the following unanswered and rather troubling questions in mind:

(1) Whose 'competitive advantage' is being sought?

(2) who is being dis-advantaged, dis-possessed, crushed, or bashed?

Practicing corporate managers, politicians and individuals cannot continue to simply ignore these questions, for the disadvantaged and dispossessed are increasing in number and 'will soon raise their voices'. Moreover, in the development of new theories of competitive strategy, the unanswered questions and the twinned ambiguities of competitiveness and entity must be studied together, with joint resolution.

Strategic entities

Despite the ambiguity and complexity, managers, politicians and model-builders are continuing to express their concerns about achieving the competitiveness of firms in what is fast becoming a world alliances and networks, or of industries, in a what has long been seen as a post-industrial society, or of national or regional economies, in what has now becoming an international or global economy. This rhetoric does not acknowledge the multiple types of strategic entity, including individuals, whose fate is increasingly intertwined and whose physically and culturally-determined boundaries are now in a state of flux. As a result of technological change, there are now a great many candidates for the 'competitive' entity, or the proper subject of the formal models and theories of competition. The multiple types of strategic-entity include:

Individuals, families and clans; sects and religions, groups, associations and coalitions; corporations, firms, organizations; business units or segments, flex-firms, hollow or virtual corporations; strategic alliances; MNCs and TNCs; strategic-groups, industries; networks, learning communities, institutions, cities regions, nations, blocs, societies or social-systems...

...as well as the global human productive enterprise viewed as a singular and unitary whole. In addition to this long list of physical entities, there are still other, more abstractly conceived candidates such as: *multiple-selves, players, cognitive—systems, living systems and autopoietic systems.*

Particular theories, models and concepts of

competition have been considered as applying to any member of this entity-set. Yet, the proper scope of application remains controversial and ambiguous, to say the least. For example, Krugman has equated competitiveness with productivity, but only in the case of large regions where most products are consumed within the entity. For traditional corporations it becomes relative market-share, with other measures. Smaller export-oriented national economies are a third distinctive case. Here, the political managers remain more directly accountable for the well—being of the electorate, or the employees, so to speak. Yet another case are learning communities and knowledge based alliances, whose 'competitive weapons' are used to achieve market dominance and to defeat ignorance.

In-sum, it is quite apparent that the traditional concepts of competitiveness, which imply warrior like attack and defence of a territory or a border, must now be updated. Technological changes have significantly undermined the factory walls, permeated the borders and even penetrated the skin of individuals, creating a growing awareness that all boundaries, even the sacred boundary of the skin, are now in a state of flux. As Yawata has noted, there are no mainstream theories that can adequately express the resulting universal problems of 'boundary maintenance, socioeconomic exchange and conditions for peaceful co-existence'. Accordingly, it has become necessary to formulate competitive-strategy in practice without any adequate understanding. One must simply tolerate the ambiguities and accept that there are multiple solutions.

Strategy-as-rationality

The conceptual framework of Strategy as Rationality offers one theoretical means of expression, for this problem. In the framework, all strategic-entities are seen to be plurally rational. Their behaviour conforms, at various times and in varying degrees to all of the forms of rationality identified in the broad spectrum of the social sciences. Put differently, all elements of the rationality-set are assumed to co-exist in all strategic entities, whose behaviour then varies according to a 'perceived multi-verse'. This framework cuts through the Gordian knot. It embraces complementariy whilst remaining fundamentally pragmatic as the twinned ambiguities of competition and entity are regarded as mere roadblocks in the path of inquiry.

This strategy-set is seen to be in isomorphic correspondence with the rationality-set. Such a frame of reference is neither blunt, blind, nor even particularly radical; since a great many of the available treatises on on strategy already assume some such correspondence, either implicitly or explicitly. For example, in recent studies of international competitiveness, as the distinctive strategies of Western vs Asian firms were interpreted as follows :

> 'Asian firms' emphasis on soft skills such as networking stands in sharp contrast to the economic-rationality of Western firms'.

'The Japanese industrial emphasis on theoretical rationality their commitment to engineering and R&D'.

Likewise, observations of the unreflective or simplified nature of many strategic decisions have often been interpreted with reference to imperfect or bounded forms of rationality. Indeed, this grand passage from the strategy—set to the rationality-set has been navigated so casually, in both directions, that it is only natural to map it out more fully.

The general theory

The general theory of rationality concerns the identification of distinctive forms of rationality together with their meta-rational relationships. Just a few elements of this rationality-set are briefly identified in Table.

The general theory involves a variety of similar meta-ration criteria and relationships, including:

- Classificatory meta-rational criteria;
- Evaluative meta-rational criteria; and
- Relational meta-rational arguments, that place the elements and subsets of the rationality set in relation to each other.

From the perspective of Strategy-as-Rationality, the theory, language and prescription of strategy is seen to be isomorphic with this general theory of rationality. Accordingly, in researching and practicing strategy, one is also engaged in re-constructing, refining or re-applying existing meta—rational relations, or else discovering new ones. Most importantly, any advances in the general theory of rationality directly inform strategy. Examples to date may be found in to the contexts of strategy-with-sunk-costs, strategy-as-moral-philosophy and strategic-intelligence, or 'competitor' analysis. The latter may now be elaborated, following an account of the new concept of hyper-rationality.

Hyper-strategy

In their studies of the international competitiveness of the Japanese industrial system, Ritzer and Le Moyne described the behaviour of that entity as a manifestation of relationships amongst some distinctive forms of rationality : formal, theoretical, practical, substantive, as described in table. These particular elements of the rationality-set are defined in the prolific works of Max Weber and his followers, so they are undoubtedly rather familiar to students of Sociology. Yet they are absent, or not explicit, in any mainsteam discourse on competitive strategy. The analysis of competitiveness in terms of these forms proceeded in three stages:

(1) mapping of the four rationalities onto their corresponding strategy-concepts.

(2) specification of some meta-rational relations, and....

(3) identification of actual and potential synergies resulting from the co-existence of these forms of rationality in a strategic entity.

Some elements of the rationality-set

Belief-oriented forms	
Theoretical (Weberian)	The entity masters reality by means of increasingly precise and abstract concepts.
Strong-intensive	The entity creates models (symbolic representations) in the process of seeking the truth about the environment, then uses the models to shape expectations.
Extensive	The entity's expectations are formed by extrapolating historical data.
Strategic	The entity's beliefs and expectations take into account the anticipated responses and interactions of other entities.
Natural	Routine self-criticism by the entity yields greater validity of its beliefs.
Open	The entity takes corrective measures in response to all of its past mistakes, as identified by itself and others.
Consensual	Beliefs reflect authentic consensus amongst entity's subsystems.
	Means-oriented forms
Formal (Weberian)	Decision processes are codified and shaped around generally applicable laws.
Practical (Weberian)	Entity seeks expedient ways of pusuing a given practical end.
Selective (environment)	Rules of survival and growth are located in the environment.

	Over time the environment selects those entities that conform to the rules.
Selective (potential)	The entity makes a trade-off between (i) a pressure to act in accordance with its capabilities and potential, against (ii) constraints perceived by the entity.
Systemic	Knowledge, goals, behavioral rules and capabilities accumulate in the entity and its environment. These must be developed over time.
Expressive (communicative)	The entity builds identity and reputation Rational actions are primarily symbolic, not instrumental
RUM	Rational Utility Maximisation. Formal rank-ordering of preferences for defined objects of choice.
	Ends-oriented
Substantive (Weberian)	The entity's choices are guided by a consistent set of ultimate human values. (H. Simon used 'substantive' as a belief-oriented form.)
Extended	The entity has goals relating to the wider social system, or theinterest of other entities, in addition to selt interest.
Sympathy	Regard for the interest of others is prudential, it enables utility maximization in social and strategic contexts.

Commitment	The entity makes counterpreferential choices, sacrificing utility for the sake of others.
Utilitarian	An entity should choose the action that will bring about the greatest good (wealth, harmony, freedom, etc.) for the greatest number (of other entities).
Expressive (identity)	The process of ambiguity reduction (deciding goals) is itself of ultimate value. It produces a sense of autonomy.
Deontology, Kantian	Performance of duties and respect for rights are of paramount importance.
	Other forms
Contextual (institutional)	An entity's actions should be oriented towards the creation and maintenance of instiutions (other enduring entities) that symbolise the good life with others.
Structural	A rational entity continually improves its own decision structure, with respect to (i) the involvement of subsystems, (ii) identification of issues, (iii) the distinguishing of phases.

Strategy - rationality correspondences

The fourWeberian forms of rationality correspond with the observed elements of Japanese industrial strategy, as follows :

- *Formal - LRP, MITI.* Bureaucratic processes like formal Long-Range Planning, along with formal structures like the Ministry of International Trade and Industry in Japan are manifestations of Weberian formal rationality, i.e., they are shaped around codified and generally applicable laws.

- *Practical - QCs, brainstorming, Ringi.* The use of quality circles, brainstorming, and 'bottom-up' suggestions, in order to meet the challenges of improved quality and new product development, are seen as examples of Weberian practical rationality, i.e, they are expedient ways of pursuing a given practical end.

- *Theoretical - knowledge acquisition, R&D-focus.* Commitments to Research and Development and the acquisition of knowledge and information, together with general education in mathematics and economics, in the wider society, are all seen as examples of Weberian theoretical rationality, i.e., mastery of reality by means of increasingly precise and abstract concepts.

- *Substantive - system values.* Relative to individualism, the values of groupism, interdependence, harmony and obligation are seen as manifestations of Weberian substantive rationality, i.e., where economic choices are guided by a consistent set of ultimate human values.

These four distinctive forms of rationality were observed to co-exist in the highly 'competitive' Japanese industrial system. In contrast, the

American industrial systems were primarily seen to be formally rational, with the other forms only weakly manifest, or completely absent. Others have independently noted that economic rationality is indeed to the fore in the strategic behavior of Western firms, but much less apparent in highly successful Asian firms.

Meta-rational relations

The next phase of the Ritzer and Le Moyne analysis noted the apparent relevance of relational meta-rational arguments to competitive strategy. For example :

- Abstract ideas help in the attainment of practical ends;
- Rules and laws are mindful of practical abilities and disposition;
- There are scientific inputs to formal administrative procedures, like LRP, JIT, statistical methods.

These phrases, such as 'help in', 'mindful of', 'inputs to', simply convey the idea that success, viability or competitiveness appears to involve something more than the mere implantation of plural rationality. There must also be some type of creative or productive interplay, interaction or synergy amongst the various forms of rationality.

Synergies

As a factor in strategic analysis, the general concept of synergy is undoubtedly familiar. For example, in the analysis of mergers and acquisitions, it is routine to adjust forecasts, such as E.P.S., in order to reflect the impact on acquirer and target of expected production or marketing synergies. More generally, any viable system must, according to Beer, be distinctly more than the sum of its independently acting 'elements' i.e., '2 + 2 = 5'. Since that times, the concept of synergy has become more closely associated with the productive integration of knowledge. For example, in corporations, knowledge-synergies have been obtained from simply bringing together groups of once-separate intelligence analysts. In Alliances, knowledge synergies are often seen as the main link between the parents.

It is but a small step from seeking knowledge-synergies in a strategic entity, to seeking rationality-synergies. Put differently, the 'elements' in Beer's definition of a viable or competitive entity could be understood as including the elements of its rationality-set. Accordingly, in the Ritzer and Le Moyne study, such synergies were identified amongst the Weberian forms, specifically, within the Japanese industrial system. Yet these researchers are most definitely not alone in their broad line of strategic thinking :

- Maruyama has been actively encouraging corporate strategists to 'figure out ways of making positive use of differences', between the 'multiple logics' that are 'present to varying degrees in different cultures'.
- Yawata has noted that 'every concrete case of capital operation in a society is a synthesis', in

which market exchange operates synergistically with other distinctive cultural historical and institutional dimensions.

- Evolutionary theorists now hold that competitive success in the natural world is a product of a dynamaic interplay between altruism, i.e., commitment, sympathy, interdependent-utility and self-interest in the behavior of various types of entity.
- In numerous other case studies 'successful' organization and social-systems have each been seen to operate in a state of creative tension, evoked by their plural-rationality, but coupled with an implicit understanding of strategy-as-synthesis.

The conceptual framework of Strategy-as-Rationality, when it is extended to include the synergy-set now provides a quite general framework into which all of these empirical observations of strategy and their local theoretical interpretations fit perfectly. By adopting the framework, it becomes quite apparent that the concept of synergy amongst forms of rationality could usefully be generalised to refer to all types of strategic entity and to all elements of the rationality-set. In the following sections, adapated methodologies of competitive strategic analysis are discussed further, together with their associated ideologies and the necessary transitions.

Methodology

The concept of competitiveness as hyperstrategy underpins new approaches to implanting competitive strategy, competitor analysis and the measurement of levels of competitiveness, as follows.

Implanting hyper strategy has two phases. First, any missing or absent elements of an entity's rationality set should be identified. For example, in any given entity, learning processes awareness of the environment, procedural fairness and respect for rights might be absent, or only weakly manifest. Efforts should then be directed at implanting these rationalities.

Some synergies amongst rationalities

Forms of rationality	*Synergies*
	Weberian forms
Theoreotical, practical	An emphasis on knowledge increases the utilisation of lower-level skills
Practical, substantive	Bottom up practical rationality is reinforced by the ethic of groupism.
Practical, formal	Bottom up ideas improve the functioning of assembly lines and bureaucracies
Theoretical, substantive	Values of groupism and harmony strengthens the commitment of scientists to contribute to the success of the entity.
Formal, substantive	Values of groupism and harmony foster the development of the permanent employment systems which, in turn, reinforces those values.

	Other forms
Expressive, RUM	Profitable exchange could be used to reinforce a sense of
Contextual, RUM	Profitable exchange could be used to strengthen a vision of the good life with others.
Resolute, kantian	A sense of duty and obligation could reinforce persistence with long standing messions.
Systemic, expressive	Lessons from the past could be used to reinforce a sense of identity and autonomy.
Scientific, extended (ends)	Formal model could be used to reinforce the values or clarify goals.
Extensive (belief), minimal	The process of forming expectations creates opportunties for activating knowledge and making new inferences.
Contextual, scientific	Appropriate institutional arrangements reinforce the link between scientific progress and financial success.
Expressive, formal	Formal reward systems in organizations can reinforce a sense of identity.
Open, commitment	Total commitment to safety improves the level of learning from mistakes and vice-versa.
Strategic, structural	Configuration of subsystems, can be adjusted to optimize the interplay of competition and co-operation.
Structural, minimal	Participation in multiple markets creates opportunities for new inferences.

It is absolutely crucial to understand that this

does not imply any displacement, or squeezing out of an entity's existing rationalities. The principle of complementarity applies. Thus the economically rational firm must also learn and seek consensus, to raise its level of competitiveness, thus defined. The individual scientist or committed altruist must also be mindful of the need to attract both customer and capital. The advocate of shareholder oriented strategies, or customer-oriented strategies must also tackle identity, poverty and social integration. Put differently, a combative attitude to creating wealth is rather futile, unless, equal attention is also devoted to commensurate political social and economic reform'. Certainly, hyper strategy is based upon the premise that all strategic-entities should 'go forth and ....be.... multiply ..... rational', rather than simply cultivate an irrational obsession with winning.

Yet implanting plural-rationality may not be enough, it is also necessary to seek out possible synergies, along the lines of the examples in Tables. For example, the financial success of an entity could be managed in ways that reinforce its sense of identity. The latter could, in turn, strengthen the commitment of scientists to contribute to its success. Missions of safety-improvement are strongly supported by an openness towards learning from mistakes. Decisions about cost-leadership or differentiation must be replaced with an imperative to seek both ways of adding value to marketed outputs. More generally, implanting hyper-strategy involves the creation of synergies and augmentations amongst plural-rationalities, thereby extending the boundaries of strategic thinking. At the same time, concerns for others are simply swept in to the process. Conventional competitive strategy, in contrast, involves trade-offs and exclusiveness.... as well as defeats and failures.

Ultra-games

One major barrier to implanting hyperstrategy in practice is the persistence of outdated models, rationalities and language. For example, to the extent that one is trained in the formal models of game theory, or oligopoly theory, it becomes that much harder to think and communicate in terms of the more elusive elements of the rationality set, i.e., the forms of rationality not easily or fully captured by RUM. Rather similar comments have been made about all formal economic models in relation to strategic management thinking.

Such persistence is especially questionable in the case of formal Game Theory, because the mathematically derived solutions have never solved any real strategic managerial problem. On the other hand, if one looks to the natural language meta-theory of GT a strikingly different picture is revealed. The meta-theory, with its associated conceptual or mental models, has been very fully accommodated into main-stream strategic management methods and language. Witness the tremendous popularity and influence of Porter's works.

If one accepts that meta-theory, mental-models or conceptual-models can properly be termed 'useful', then the same can now surely be said of a conceptual model of a competitive game where strategic interactions are seen to occur between large numbers of hyper-rational entities, rather than the utility maximising players of GT. Accordingly, a conceptual model of an Ultra-game should now be developed, where each entity is seen to be engaged not only in a bounded search for utility maximisation, but in a much broader search for success, with reference to plural rationality and multiple synergies. In Ultra-games, each 'player' operates in a complex and dynamic world, a multi-verse, with attentional limits, constrained autonomy, coherent vision and concerns for human betterment.

This 'theory' is, to be sure, nothing more than a conceptual or mental model, expressed in the fuzzy categories of natural language. The theory of Ultra-games might be stated more formally, but, in truth,it is not at all necessary to solve, nor even to formulate an Ultra-game! This is because the lines of inquiry set out in Table represent meta-theory, in two distinct senses. First, they are expressed in natural language so they can directly influence conceptual or mental models rather than report mathematical inferences. Second, the methodology integrates diverse theories. Nonetheless, as meta-theory, Ultra-games could find practical application in competitive strategic management contexts, quite directly. Players in the Ultra-game must simply ask important questions, rather than find mathematical solutions to their strategic problems.

Strategic analysis sing Ultra-games

A. *Some inquiries about rationalities*

1. What are the entity's...
   - expectations about our behavior?
   - rules and procedures?
   - internal incentive structures?
   - stated goals?
   - capabilities?
   - actual and potential level of performance? etc.

. Does the entity....
   - use a model-based forecasting system?
   - use social cost-benefit analysis?
   - balance stockholder interests?
   - have a history or policy of treating others fairly?
   - preserve traditions?
   - contribute to the development of institutions that symbolise a good life with others?
   - respect and promote rights of others etc.

3. Is there a pattern over time in the entity's activities?

4. What are the observer's (.eg. analyst's biases?

B. *Some inquiries about synergies*

1. Weberian. Does the entity.....
   - apply scientific knowledge to increase the utilisation of its lower level human skills?
   - utilise experience at all levels to continually improve its own processes?
2. *Other. Does the entity.....*
   - persist with long standing missions because of a sense of duty?
   - reinforce its own values by using appropriate formal models?
   - use incentive systems in ways that build a sense of identity?
   - take opportunities for creative inference, arising from its involvement in multiple contexts?

- attempt to configure its subsystems to optimise interplay of competition and cooperation?
- learn from mistakes in order to increase its commitment to a mission?
- apply reflective thinking with justice concerns to its strategic behavior?
- strengthen its identity by forging links with benevolent institutions?
- Use extrapolatory forecasting processes as platforms for accessing knowledge and making inferences? etc.

Towards Mesurement

For those who insist upon quantification and measurement in strategic analysis, ways might be foud. Certainly there are several ways to measure conventional forms of synergy, as well as the potential performance of firms and industries. One such approach was suggested by Beer and subsequently elaborated in the PARE methodology But how many are now using these measurements? More recently. The International Competitiveness Model which measures actual and potential competitiveness as a function of many parameters, has been successfully applied to corporate strategy formulation. With hyperstrategy now in mind, the level of competitiveness could be reformulated as the combined magnitude of the synergies amongst the rationality set of an entity. As with all other model based measures of competitiveness, the operational details would have to be worked out to suit each unique context.

Ideologies

Why should any strategic entity attempt to implement hyper-strategy, use ultra games or attempt to measure synergies? The answer to this question lies in the limitations and paradoxes inherent in the traditional models, rationalities and language of competition. When these are acted upon by many entities, the inevitable outcome is that Losers and even entire loser nations and states, are spawned in abundance. Put differently, if every strategic entity is trying to achieve competitiveness only by winning market dominance and beating others, great and widespread harm is done, whilst only a few entities can in fact succeed. Moreover, these few often do so quite spectacularly. This is because the weak does not become stronger by freely competing with the strong: he is simply crushed. The reality of an obsession with competitiveness as winning, then as has been amply demonstrated throughout human history, is more injustice, more oppression more dislocation increased disparity and envy, increased poverty and frustration, more environmental destruction and more war.

Despite this, with current Zeitgeist, it has become all too easy for corporate managers and national politicians to win social and political approval of a harmful proposal, simply demonstrating that (it) is necessary for meeting competitive challenges. All too often corporate downsizing and re-engineering, are mere short term tactical responses that neglect human motivation organizational learning product innovation and social dislocation. This capability and gullibility is by n means confined to the contemporary US corporate scene. At least some

Asian industrial entities have recently claimed that Americans are trying to impose Western standards? Nothing more than basic *dignity* and modest *freedoms* for all. Yet, despite such hardships, in order to make Asian products less competitive. And what one might ask, are those tricky Western standards the need to 'achieve international competitiveness' continues to be upheld as a quasi moral imperative for all entities all over the world.

Rhetoric

One might attempt a resolution of this paradox by drawing a crisp distinction between rhetoric and a more complex reality. For example, Krugman has recently noted that the rhetoric of competitiveness-as-winning can be exciting, motivating, perhaps even productive, even though the true nature of success and failure is far more complex. Yet this is really no resolution at all. In fact, rhetoric (in) forms the environment, gradually making it more benign, fertile and rich... or, alternatively, more hostile, arid and tough. If a rose is re-named at 'thistle' it will be weeded out. Thus, the unfettered and incessant rhetoric of competitiveness-as-winning has indeed become a dangerous obsession. Accordingly, a more enlightened rhetoric is urgently needed; one that is capable of accommodating complexity, co-evolution, and harmony .... in addition, of course, to supporting efficient exchanges.

Meta-criteria

This search for enlightened rhetoric is also, at the

same time, a search for rationality. This is because the language and conceptual categories of strategic management can be evaluated with direct reference to meta-rational criteria. For example, when compared with the crude rhetoric of competitiveness-as-winning the language of hyperstrategy is itself:

- *Universalizable:* each entity would prefer all other entities to use the language and to implant hyperstrategy. In contrast, one cannot coherently speak of all entities having an Advantage'. A niche perhaps but not an advantage.
- *Agent oriented:* the language of hyperstategy speaks directly to all entities themselves. It does not exclusively target the powerful, nor the designers of any system, or nation.
- *Elusive:* The full meaning of hyper-strategy cannot be adequately conveyed by any single criterion. Any tradeoffs amongst elements are much less important than augmentations and synergies.

The language of hypers-tategy appears, thus, to satisfy some important evaluative meta-rational criteria. Achieving competitivenss thus defined, no longer means seeking advantage and disadvantage. Rather efforts directed at implanting hyper-strategy and playing ultra-games are far more likely to foster an appreciation f complexity, thereby helping all entities to see the world as it really is:

Adaptations and transitions

It is one thing to espouse an alternative rhetoric and ideology of competitiveness, but quite another to bring about transitions from the old to the new. One approach to ideological transition could be to link it to the concept of methodological adaptation. For example the methodology of Ultra games could be quite fairly described as an adaptation of the competitive strategy techniques associated with Game theory. Next, an explicit link between such methodological adaptation and a corresponding ideological transition may be forged by invoking the concepts of Decision Function Rationality and then referring to the isomorphism between strategy and rationality.

Decision Function Rationality is simply a mapping that associates any given model or method with its implicit form(s) of rationality. For examples traditional competitor analysis techniques have implicitly assumed economic rationalities. Game theory assumes utility maximisation, with its several RUM captured variants, such as intensive and extensive, weak and strong. Accordingly, one could write:

The international Competitiveness Model also implicitly assumes selective rationality because considerations of potential performance, competition, and maximisation are all present in applications of that particular model.

Most notably, with the implementation of the ICM the mental models were also extended to incorporate considerations of potentiality into their strategic thinking. Similar but broader changes could now flow from attempts to implement Ultra games as methodology. In this case, the range of the mapping D is the rationality set R, united with the synergy set Y. Thus one could write:

The process of methodological adaptation (i,e. games to ultra games) is now seen to corresponds to a transition (1) from economic-rationality to plural rationality, together with (ii) an accompanying ideological transition, from the outdated language of competitive strategy, to the newer categories of meaning involved in hyperstategy. In adapting methodology, terms like winnters and losers maximization, or market system also become supplanted with notions of co existence, synergies, respecty and human systems.

The structure illustrated is by no means exclusive to models and concepts of competitiveness competition and competitive strategy. Other similar examples of methodological adaptations include:

- *Fakecasting as an adaptation of DGF methodology:* DCF may be adapted to become a device for evoking knowledge.
- *De Novo programming as an adaptation of MCDM:* Multicriteria decision models may be adapted to incorporate the explicit design of alternatives and the selection of decision criteria thereby elaborating concepts of optimality.
- *MDA as an adaptation of DA :* Traditional decision analysis, may be adapted to meta-

decision analysis, or stepping-back ... into the domain of the three meta-decisions (a) choice of strategy description. (b) choice of rationalities, and (c) choice of models.

The obvious question about any links between methodology and ideology is: 'Which comes first?' Normally, methodologies are developed after ideologies are well in truly in place. Yet, for transitions, this temporal or causal sequence might usefully be put into reverse. One might first change an entity's behavior and then wait patiently for corresponding transitions in rationalities and ideologies to occur, over time. The suggestion 'adapt now and re-think later' is, in fact, nothing other than the familiar principle of behavior modification in clinical Psychology. Although the latter may not have been intended as a grand theory of ideological transitions, it could now be a very good reason to implement Ultra-games.

3 Strategy Design Tradeoffs-Free

Introduction

In the early development of management systems, a few generally accepted principles contended with the tightly knit community of business researchers and practitioners who worked by intuition and folklore, and by drawing on ideas and research from military strategy, political science, economics, marketing and organizational sociology and psychology. To reduce this intellectual chaos, Anthony proposed a conceptual framework which according to Hax and Candea and Wiseman was destined to achieve a paradigm status. Anthony's framework decomposed managerial decision making into three parts: strategic planning, tactical planning, and operational control. Resembling Bouldings hierarchy of complexity, these parts form a system hierarchy, with strategic planning at the top and operational control at the bottom, along several dimensions: time horizon, management level, value of judgment, and decision importance.

Under the supposition that production entails

simple and restricted activities. Anthony wished to minimize top managers intervention in operations and to transfer decision making authority from staff to line managers. Moved by these objectives, several of his colleagues and disciples were already using Anthony's framework to guide their research when his book first appeared in 1965. Soon his paradigm permeated management systems and, by fragmenting and over simplifying their complexity, it isolated production from strategic management. This segregation has blocked operational research from penetrating the strategic apex despite its enormous success at logistics support. Presently, the growing awareness that strategic management is tending to greater interdependence with production and the danger of system performance deterioration owed to maximizing sub-systems call for a conceptual re-integration of management systems.

To overcome the dysfunctional effects of Anthony's paradigm on management systems, this essay enacts Shingos conceptual breakthrough that depicts production as a well-specified net of processes and operations. A unique visualization with practical implications for production Shingos framework not only helps unearth and negate the dysfunctional effects of Anthony's paradigm on management systems but also leads to an isomorphic representation—a new framework of strategic management as a well specified net of strategies and tactics. Paralleling the new framework, the widely publicized moves at Daimler Benz illustrate how firms design effective goal seeking strategies efficiently through the flexible coalignment of tactics.

Extending Shingos breakthrough to strategic management requires juxtaposing the conventional view of production and strategic management and their network representation toward a tradeoffs free synthesis of management systems—a trademark of modern management. The extensions contribution embodies a dynamic view of strategy that can narrow or bridge even the indomitable gap between strategy and production.

Dysfunctional effects

Dysfunctional Production Production researchers, who ordinarily welcome conceptual diversity as a way of advancing their field, resolutely endorse the strategic positioning of production as an out come that can lead firms to sustainable profits. Within the production strategy field, however, some researchers view diversity as dysfunctional, fearing that by ignoring the strategic management literature production research may stand the risk of reinventing the wheel. Consequently, they strive to coalesce well established ideas into a growing base of theory, urge colleagues to integrate the two literatures, and try to advance the production strategy field to its potential despite existing semantic differences.

Semantic differences repel managers who seek quick benefits from and try to implement production strategies through an ill-structured, behavioral approach. Soon, they focus on infrastructure, culture, and managerial styles. Only to find themselves reacting to corporate and business strategies, with marketing taking a boundary spanning role between a firms production and its competitors and customers. Infrastructure is vital to successful implementation but production strategy usually fails when its design gets bypassed. Paying no attention to design assumes that design is merely perfunctory or self-fulfilling—both in an analytical and in an organizational sense-once corporate goals have been established. Marucheck et al. argue that this has not been the case in the corporate, business, or marketing strategy research and it should not be the case in operations strategy.

The assumption they unearth parallels that of Anthony's on the simplicity of production activities but, while assuming that the design of production strategy is perfunctory or self-fulfilling is dysfunctional, the second oversimplification effect of Anthony's paradigm is even more so. It lurks behind the traditional representation of production processes and operations as overlapping phenomena lying on a single dimension sharing Anthonys objectives, production writers have been too quick to contend that the primary difference between the two lies in the scale of action depending on the research perspective or context, process is the large unit of analysis and operation is the small one.

The linear representation implies that production performance will improve operations the small units of analysis—improve. Some production researchers hold the more obscure notion that, if operations improved, processes the large units of analysis would also improve. This unidimensional perspective also reflects Anthonys assumption of simple and restricted activities in production. Though compelling it blocks theory building and keeps production strategy an underdeveloped field, inextricably bound up by its tautological definition: a strategy for production a part of business strategy or strongly integrate with the business and corporate strategies.

Dysfunctional strategy

Lurking behind the unidimensional view of Anthony's oversimplification has infected not only strategic management but organization theory too. Among the five organizational parts that Mintzberg delineates, for example, the strategic apex is connected by a flaring middle line to the operating core. Indicating a single line of top-down authority, these parts constitute nothing more than cheap linguistic makeup artfully applied on Anthony's framework - cheap 'language games'.

The oversimplification effect is most clearly visible in Quinn's rendition of strategies versus tactics, where he states that the primary difference between the two 'lies in the scale of action or the perspective of the leader'. Perfectly isomorphic to the conventional representation of production, matches Quinn's linear thinking about strategic management: depending on one's perspective or scale of action, both describe strategy as the large unit of analysis in strategic management and tactic as the small one.

The evidence on the oversimplification effects of Anthony's paradigm accounts for much of the attention and ink devoted to pinning strategic management down, and to narrowing it, as in Porter's dogmatism of generic strategies, in order to make some elbow-room for the creator, proselytizer, idealist, bricoleur, and diviner visionaries of Westley and Mintzberg unidimensional five-cell typology of strategic leadership that emerged from the clinical study of five leaders. Again limited to the five toes of the human foot and by linear thinking, Mintzberg's Five Ps for strategy' is another good example of dysfunctional theorizing which, according to Samuelson, can cretinize strategic management. Turning inductive theorizing into an artful epistemology of 'typing', along with a destructive emphasis on epiphenomena, both in the name of linking the richness of theory with the richness of practice, often project strategic management as a pseudo-skill, a costly credential that business students waste their time and money learning. This 'linking' is precisely what production researchers and managers - in their genuine quest for knowledge - have been looking for but in the wrong direction.

Shingo's breakthrough

Quite common in production research has become the utterance of terms such as 'distinctive competence', 'mission', 'strategy', and 'task'.

However, is a definite amount of work of Webster but, to Skinner, a broad notion akin to manufacturing strategy itself. Evidently, Skinner has wedged the semantic difference battle in the wrong direction. According to Taylor, Webster wins this one: production includes activity tasks or bundles leading from raw material to finished goods or services. If the task of production is to deliver a specific good or service, then a process can be designed to so do by selecting two or more among four principal operations: work activity, inspection, transports, and storage. In production operations contain activity bundles, sometimes called therbligs.

Although the conventional view of production discounts the difference between operations and processes, it is perfectly natural for the directly - observable motion of operational activities to capture the attention of production researchers, manages, and journalists - particularly those who are not sensitized to this difference. Some may even conclude the production consists exclusively of operations. However, production involves two distinct streams of activity: operations depict the activity of workers and machines; from raw material to finished goods and services.

The idea that process improvements can greatly improve production performance, and to a much higher level than secondary operational improvements can, is far from being well understood.

In production, superior performance demands process improvements

According to Shingo, firms attain production goals through process improvements; operations play a supplementary role. For example, a conveyor improves a transportation operation rather than transportation. Similarly, a fully-automated warehouse—a multimillion-dollar investment-improves an inventory operation rather than inventory. The improvement of a production process that incorporates transportation and inventory operations can eliminate the need for conveyors and automated warehouses altogether.

Production is a net of processes and operations along two distinct streams of activity. To improve production performance, researchers and managers must emphasize process improvements before operational ones. Drawing a clear distinction between operations and processes is a fundamental step toward breaking free from the segregation effects of Anthony's paradigm on management systems. Redesigning production processes to enable a tadeoffs-free corporate-, business—or functional-level strategy requires creativity—a prerequisite to innovation. The enabling stems from decision alternatives that put a firm's strategic planning team on the spot: having to decide which benefit to promote first among high-quality products and services, high efficiency, high flexibility, and supersonic speed of delivery leads to a good market position no matter what the strategy level.

Strategic management: A net view

Strategic management has also advanced despite

existing semantic differences but its terminology is as confusing as that of production and its content as ill-defined too. Anthony's paradigm has permeated strategy research deeply, resulting in linear thinking that does short-shrift questions concerning the essence of strategic management. Conceptual clarity perhaps can stop the vain pursuit of will-of-the-wisp questions, so that strategy researchers stand up the field's recalcitrant issue of designing effective strategies and tactics.

Although the conventional view of strategic management discounts the difference between strategy and tactics, it is perfectly natural for the highly visible moves of tactics to capture the attention of strategy researchers, managers, and students—particularly those who are not sensitized to this difference. Some may even conclude that strategic management consists exclusively of collective or competitive tactics. However, strategic managements does involve two distinct streams of activity: the design and implementation of strategies, and the design and implementation of tactics.

Strategies aim at achieving a firm's superordinate goals, i.e., sustainable profits over time. Implementing a strategy requires designing and implementing tactics. In turn, the design of each tactic entails deciding whether it will be collective or competitive; and action or communication. The horizontal axis of characterizes the behavioural nature of tactics, ranging from entirely accommodative to collective to neutral to competitive to entirely adverse. The vertical axis characterizes the physical nature of tactics, ranging from the pure communication to pure action. Extending Shingo's breakthrough to strategic management is simply a matter of realizing that individuals, groups, and organizations design goal-seeking strategies by combining two or·more among the four tactics cast into the four quadrants.

The best strategies combine collective and competitive tactics, and mix action with pure communication moves. Typically, a structural move costs much more to reverse in a single instance than communication but repeated communication reversals lead to lost credibility. In the late 1970s, for example, the Israelis could only have reversed their accommodative tactic of evacuating the Sinaï Desert by force and a high cost. However, their subsequent adverse communique that they would have had reoccupied the territory unless Egypt reciprocated, would not necessarily involve a significant cost if reversed. That two-tactic strategy ended an ugly war.

In today's new realities, any firm, industry country or world region that subscribes exclusively either to competition or to collectivism must expect to perform contrary to its objectives. Exclusive emphasis on competitive tactics leads to adversity, which defies the benefits of competition. Similarly, a bias for collectivism leads to accommodative protectionism, which deprives firms and industries from the critical mass of production output and sales they collectively need to survive. The intersecting Y_js and X_is of th figure depict strategic management as a well-defined network of goal-seeking strategies implemented through the timed coalignment of collective and competitive tactics. The need to design strategies aimed at achieving the superordinate goals of customer satisfaction and transnational reciprocity is self evident to the participants of the transnational economy, which germinates as firms learn to design their future.

The new framework depicts strategic management as a net of strategies and tactics along two distinct steams of activity: goal-seeking strategies implemented through collective and competitive tactics that mix pure action with communication. To improve firm performance, researchers and managers must stress the improvement of strategies more than the improvement of tactics. Drawing a clear distinction between strategies and tactics is a fundamental step toward breaking free from the segregation effects of Anthony's paradigm on management systems. And breaking free is a prerequisite to designing strategies and tactics tradeoffs-free.

In strategy, superior implementation demands superior design

Implies that although piecemeal tactics can undermine strategy, they are secondary. Even if a single-tactic strategy were feasible, a superior design would entail an efficient strategy that expels counterproductive tacties. Examples of counter-productive tactics are those coercive moves that increase rivalry among existing competitors without a real payoff, either direct or indirect, for the industry incumbent who initiates such moves. It is a typical of an industry or market leader to initiate such coercive moves.

A firm's superordinate goal is not simply to compete but to develop its capability of creating unique ways to serving its current and future customers. Neither can firms expect to drift into a strategy design but must move beyond copying and learn to design strategies. The conventional perspective of copycat strategy shows linear thinking at best and clumsy benchmarking - also known as shadow marketing - at worst. Its proponents assume that they can improve long-term performance incrementally, i.e, with disconnected tactical moves alone, when improvements in strategy design should be their primary concern.

A more cautious approach leads to logical incrementalism, where changes in strategy derive from the combined state vector of a firm's current strategy and the industry environment. In a stable environment, if the proximity or fit between the firm's current strategy and the environment is high,then logical incrementalism may work. That is, assuming that firm performance depends only on current affairs or on the most recent past. Usually, of course, this is more of a dearly held assumption than a cold fact. When the environment becomes challenging, successful firms engage in strategic intelligence.

Recognizing the politics of planning also helps

but tactics grounded exclusively on the psychology of participation or on office politics may falter for two reasons: the trades-off bias for either collective or competitive tactics is the first reason; haste is the second. Sometimes managers fall in the trap of rushing through strategy making, shifting their attention away from time-consuming minutiae, such as strategy design. Ironically, then, they end up wasting the resource they are trying to save - time.

Strategy design usually begins by identifying variables pertinent to a firm's strategic situation, along with their casual interrelationships. Potentially, changes in these variables can have profound effects on performance. Some of the variables belong to a firm's external environment. Examples are the intensity of competition, the emergence of new products and production technologies, government regulation, and international interest and currency rates. Changes in these and other variables determine a firm's performance over time, depending on how well its managers understand the causal linkages underlying their strategic situation.

Some of the changes in pertinent variables are within a firm's control, a consequence of prevailing policies and managerial decisions. Pulling on or pushing these internal levers requires the interactive design of implementation tactics that affect performance through a dynamic chain reaction - a whole sequence of events. Sometimes it helps managers to distinguish between market and non-market variables among environmental and decision variables, particularly in institutions whose strategies entails aspects of political economy and administrative legislation. To evaluate a change in strategy, the results of designing and implementing a sequence of tactics must be anticipated, considered along with changes in a firm's environment and with respect to the firm's matching capabilities, stakeholder concerns, and organizational goals.

Strategy and production dynamics: the traditional split insuperable

Often obscure and difficult to verify, uncertain strategic outcomes cause managers to oversimplify the complex interrelationships among pertinent variables, and therefore end up ignoring the combined effects of chain reactions altogether. Unwarranted oversimplification frequently results from well-intended rationality but cognitive biases mislead decision makers. In the presence of scale economies, for example, prevailing prices alone cannot determine a firm's efficient production scale. In strategy, the scale of production itself is a design variable because it meets the two conditions which Milgrom and Roberts delineate: (a) it has predictable implications for various organization functions, and (b) the mistakes associated with incorrect perceptions of it can be serious.

Depending on the sales volume that a firm anticipates, it will adjust its sales force, supplies and distribution, equipment, and facilities to match the scale of its production. Coherent and consistent tactics designed by its production, marketing, personnel, distribution, and procurement managers demand a shared visions intended production scale over time. Sharing common perceptions about strategy dynamics is an important step toward coordinating implementation plans and managerial behavior and precisely what the new view of strategic management as a net of strategies and tactics can help a firm accomplish.

The anticipated scale of production affects more than just the scale of other functions. In the cases of GM and Toyota, the degree of outsourcing shows how production scale also determines specialization. Smaller firms, operating without specialized equipment, typically rely on suppliers for even more components when the suppliers enjoy economies of scale of their own by serving many firms. The use of specialized capital equipment makes vertical integration strategies more profitable for large firms than for small competitors. Economies of scale permit reduced production cost, which is an important element in determining price dynamics. Over time, low marginal cost allows lowering prices, which increase demand for a firm's products and services, which in turn supports increased production.

Firms can enjoy economies of scale even when they are producing at too small a sclae in a market that is too small for them but can make product components for multiple markets. GE enjoys economies of scale in small electric motors, for example, when it uses the same motors in food processors, hair dryers, fans, and vacuum cleaners. CASIO enjoys economies of scale in liquid crystal displays, which it uses to produce electronic address books, calculators, and music keyboards. The falling cost of producing LCDs led to penetrating multiple segments of the market for digital and analog wrist watches that use LCDs. Under these circumstances, firms enjoy economies of scope by producing several products together at less cost than single-product firms. Economies of scope offer the same strategy design and decision coordination benefits that economies of scale do.

The same debacles also apply. For example, meandering into a multitude of sidelines that share unique material of manufacturing techniques with Yamaha's core business has brought the firm into unfamiliar markets, with multiple environmental forces. Blithely obscured by its high-rivalry tactics in the television, VCR, and audio equipment industries, the cumulative effect of these forces has been a 30 per cent decrease in Yamaha's profits from 1990 to 1992.

Strategy design at daimler-benz

Paralleling the new strategic management framework of the highly publicized moves of Daimler-Benz puzzle the tradeoffs-biased proponents of exclusively collective or competitive tactics. Like their Israeli counterparts, the strategic-decision makers of Daimler combine collective and competitive tactics, and mix structural moves with pure communication to supplant classical-market branches with non-market modes of production. The tradeoffs-free coalignment of collective and competitive tactics enabled the late Alfred Herrhausen, CEO of Deutsche Bank, and Edzard Reuter, CEO of Daimler-Benz, to design a vast transaction network both effectively and efficiently as barriers to entry gave way to contestable markets.

Deutsche Bank's 28.5 per cent holding of Daimler was the structural move that enabled Herrhausen and Reuter to design the necessary timed coalignment of collective and competitive tactics, including a whole array of merger and acquisitions that would prepare Daimler to meet its superordinate strategic goals of customer satisfaction and transnational reciprocity. Deutsche Bank had just diversified into mortgages and insurance to offer a wide range of services its existing customers. The logic behind the Herrhausen-Reuter tradeoffs-free design was that both banking and carmaking are global industries a spread of production activities should help them both.

M&As represent expeditious ways to keeping pace with change, particularly when firms seek unique production capabilities. Alternatively, pursuing cooperation because of reciprocal dependencies may cause firms to opt for contract based governance. The contract-based governance forms that firms use because of reciprocal dependencies include strategic alliances, partnerships, coalitions, franchises, research consortia and network organizations.

The second structural move in entailed a 75 per cent acquisition of AEG, a German electronics and defense company, which had paid US$ 290M for the production automation system of Gould, a US firm. this represented a step toward the factory of the future as well as more production capacity in the United States. At the same time, Reuter hired McKinsey, a US consulting firm, to help steamline and reorganize production, so that Daimler could produce compact Mercedes cars to fend off its long-time rival, BMW, which had recently entered Daimler's luxury-car niche.

It was unclear to industry observers whether Daimler should integrate AEG into the car business or keep it as a separate industrial group. AEG offered a wide range of products from defense equipment to washing machines. In the two fields closest to Daimler, automotive electronics and production automation, AEG lagged behind its major competitors Bosch and Siemens, both suppliers of Daimler. consequently, the AEG M&A was a coercive tactical move. Yet, if the M&A were a vertical integration move, then Reuter should have had dismembered AEG and distributed the parts to each of the core firm's production functions. If it were a horizontal diversification move, then he should have left AEG alone.

Reuter's own rational behind the M&A with AEG was two-fold: to bring in-house production expertise in the increasingly important field of electronics, and to satisfy the need for a broad spread of high-technology activities under the bestcar sales flag. Indeed, Daimler needed to improve the quality of the electronic components for its luxury cars, particularly if advanced electronics were to become a critical capability in automotive production. It could learn from and use the output of electronics production to build better cars. This rationale suggested that the AEG merger was a vertical integratiion tactic. Reuter not only did not dismember AEG, however, but following Drucker's primary rule of successful acquisition, the acquiring Daimler helped its AEG target with cash and time invested in both product and process R&D.

The fourth set of tactics in the figure combined a structural move with communication. The structural move was an accommodative 65 per cent stake in Dornier, a family-owned aerospace firm. Reuters subsequent communique was an offer by Dornier to buy MBB, if the former West-German government continued covering the financial risk of the Airbus project, the German portion of which was housed in MBB. This was an adverse tactic that would bring Daimler face to face with Boeing, which can be as a B-52 bomber when it comes to fight. Yet the move was also an accommodative tactic towards the former West German government that wished to shed off its financial trauma of MBB.

The question mark shows Reuters conditional offer for MBB, while two simple payoff matrices depict the implications of his request for a continued Airbus subsidy. Given the low contestability of the global commercial-aircraft market, if both Airbus and Boeing participate at their full production capacity, then both might lose. This is exactly what the payoff matrix. Within each cell of the matrix, the upper-right corner shows the potential payoff for Airbus if it participates or not, and the lower-left corner shows the potential pay-off for Boeing if it participates or not. Conversely, the payoff matrix shows what could happen if the Airbus project were subsidized. Ceteris paribus, with a subsidy of, say, 10, Boeing stood to lose, while Airbus would be making a sustainable profit.

The situation remained unchanged until the presidential election in the United States. Three days after the election that made Mr. George Bush the president elect, the former West-German government announced MBB's privatization. Chances were slim that a republican president would subsidized Boeing. However, Daimler paid for the MBB M&A by selling off Gould to Nippon Mining, Japan, which gave the former Bush administration a chance to support Boeing with a lawsuit. The US internal revenue service (IRS) brought a lawsuit against Daimler for not having paid taxes on the Gould-nippon Miningtransaction. That coercive tactic bought Boeing some time but, naturally, te issue of jurisdiction arose because no money ever changed hands for that transaction on US soil.

The aftermath of the coalignment of tactics toward strategic goals is Deutsche Aerospace, the aircraft division of the Daimler-Benz group that recently took control of Holland's Fokker. The

Herrhausen-Reter strategy design proved to be so robust that, even without Herrhausen, Reuter was able to coalign its tactics. Boeing had no choice but to invite Deutsche Aerospace to collaborate in setting up 'a feasibility study into jointly developing a 550 to 800 seat aircraft that could enter service early next century'. The United States' long-standing complaints about Airbus subsidies were finally resolved in 1992, with an agreement limiting future government support for Airbus. However, the Bush-IRS lawsuit turn the top managers of the Daimler-Benz group into true masters of flexible accounting rules that yield 'less revealed profit and lower tax bill'. How Daimler may choose to exploit its newly-acquired unique capability is entirely up to Mr. Edzard Reuter and his successor(s).

World markets have come to expect high variety in goods and services. Dedicated production lines with long changeover times and long queues of dedicated customers are no longer viable options because they lead to much downtime and passive customer contact, respectively. Although firms acknowledge the need for change, piecemeal improvements are not only inadequate but also dangerous. In production, process reengineering helps to analyze what is made or served and how. Likewise, in strategy, scenario-driven planning helps to improve both the content and the process of strategy design and implementation.

Despite claims, however, the production strategy field is far from well developed. Its terminology is confusing and its content ill-defined. Its sorry state is palpable in the utterance of terms like 'manufacturing strategy' for goods and 'operations strategy' for services -distinction that, if taken seriously, might compel one to say that 'production strategy' is for...... the birds. The breakthrough by Shingo to depict production as a net of well-specified processes and operations is a unique visualization that greatly improves the way production researchers and managers talk about production and production strategy-neither of which is unique either to goods or to services.

To negate the dysfunctional effects of Anthony's paradigm on management systems, Shingo's framework enacted an antithesis to the traditional view of the relationship between processes and operations, and to the isomorphic counterpart of this relationship that has been posited between strategies and tactics. Shingo's breakthrough not only helped unearth and negate the dysfunctional effects of Anthony's paradigm on management systems but also helped create a new framework, an isomorphic view of strategic management as a well-specified net of strategies and tactics. Paralleling the new framework, the widely publicized moves of Daimler-Benz told how firms design effective goal-seeking strategies efficiently through the flexible coalignment of collective and competitive tactics that mix pure action with communication.

Extending Shingo's framework to strategic management was a matter of realizing that individuals, groups, and organizations design goal seeking strategies by combining two or more among the four tactics. Using collective and competitive tactics that mix structural moves and pure communication is in perfect syzygy with the plural rationality that Singer finds in individuals, groups, and organizations. Singer contrasts monothematic conventional universes of traditional rationality with the multiverse directed view of modern plural rationality. In counterpoint, Morecrofts system dynamics model of a sales organization traces the dysfunctional interactions among sales objectives, overtime, and salesforce motivation to the intended singular rationality that permeated thinking and decision making at that firm.

Because their superordinate goal is neither to compete nor to collaborate but to develop new capabilities of creating unique ways to serving their customers, firms can benefit from the multiverse directed visualization of strategic management as a well specified net of strategies and tactics. The plural rationality behind the flexible coalignment of collective and competitive tactics that mix pure action with communication can help a firm break free from the traditional tradeoffs tyranny of the mass-production era. Evidently, adherents to tradeoffs free, management like Bell Atlantic, Daimler Benz, Hallmark and Motorola can have it all.

The new framework of delineates the management of tension between competition and cooperation that becomes a fundamental condition along an industry's life cycle: depending on production capabilities firms need both strong competitors and powerful allies to market products and services. Extending Shingos breakthrough to strategic management allows focusing managerial attention on efficient strategy designs in order to eliminate tactics that unnecessarily increase adversity or protectionism. This extensions attention shifting capability toward a dynamic view of strategy can help to narrow, to bridge even the indomitable gap between strategy and production dynamics where economic paradigms and theories are rich.

Although the capabilities development and tradeoffs free management ideas originated in the context of production strategy the plurally rational view of strategic management as a net of strategies and tactics can help recast these ideas as having broad implications for strategy making. For example,the net view of strategic management gives a new meaning to Mintzbergs deliberate emergent realized and unrealized modes of business conduct. Together a well understood shared perception of a strategic situation, and interactive design and implementation of collective and competitive tactics toward broadly conceived purposes should enable a deliberate strategy design to become realized over time. Conversely, an emergent strategy design would have to depend exclusively on broadly conceived purposes, with inadequate information and misunderstood perceptions of the structure behind the strategic situation under consideration.

Even with interactive design and implementation of tactics, a small likelihood still exists that firms hoping for an emergent strategy will survive long enough to see it realized. Likewise as the world economy moves closer to a highly interconnected state of transnational reciprocity and as firms learn to design strategy and tactics a large likelihood exists for the emergent-strategy mode to become the unrealized one. The worlds new economic political and social realities make the deliberate mode of strategic management the preferred one.

4 Organizational Problem Solving

Introduction

The two previous papers in this series contained a description of the Organizational Level Learning Model and the Organizational Diagnostic Survey (ODS) Process. This paper provides a discussion of how the Organizational Diagnostic Survey Process assists in solving organizational problems. It also fleshes out more information about the methods used in the ODS Process.

Diagnosing an organization is a detective game of sifting through many conflicting clues in order to pinpoint and solve the critical organizational problems. The purpose of an organizational diagnosis is to guide problem solving to enable an organization to achieve its strategic direction and to improve its effectiveness.

There are five main issues that require explanation and integration in understanding the problem solving during the ODS Process. These are (a) incorporating the organization's context into the analysis; (b) dealing with multiple levels of organizational problems: (c) handling multiple sources of information; (d) colligating or synthesizing these into a reasonable explanation or story; and (e) developing recommended solutions and guiding the intervention to implement them.

Incorporating context

One acquires information and data from many sources while engaging in an organizational diagnosis. Data are not the same as results because results embody the integration of data. For example, using the ODS instrument, one obtains judgments from each individual completing it. These are combined to yield results in the form of measures for the six Desired Organizational Characteristics, the twelve Main Enabling Processes, the 77 Key Implementing Process the 20 Holonomic Principles, organizational knowledge, organizational learning, and even the organizational I.Q. Converting data into such results is a routine matter given the theory and the supporting ODS software. However, results, even as rich as these, are not the same as conclusions. Conclusions summarize the results in order to provide more information relative to some purpose and conditions within the organization. The shift from results to conclusions incorporates some contextual information about the organization. But conclusions are not recommendations. Recommendations involve making decisions about the meaning of the conclusions in terms of what needs to be done to solve the identified problems. Recommendations must consider the conclusions plus the capabilities and constraints facing the organization which affect its ability to solve its problems. Making recommendations involve much more contextual analysis than reaching conclusions. To go futher along this line of reasoning, recommendations are not the same as proposals. Proposals go beyond recommendations to specify how the recommendations can be converted into implementable results. Proposals incorporate even more detail about the specific organization context. For example, what resources can be expended, by whom, and according to what schedule? The proposed solution is, of course, not the same as an implemented solution which involves even more specific contextual information. Finally, an implemented solution needs to undergo an audit and review process to ascertain whether or not the solution was, in fact, ever implemented and whether or not the implemented solution actually produced the promised outcomes.

Basically as one moves from data to results to conclusions to recommendations to proposals to implemented solutions to an audit and review of the outcomes, the reliance on specific contextual factors increases and the reliance on 'objective' data decreases. Judgment and experience become more salient as one moves from data to the audit and review of the outcomes.

Levels of organizational problems

A vexing class of issues for anyone performing an organizational diagnosis is finding the set of problems. Problem solving is conceptually relatively easy compared with problem finding. The classical statistical problems of Type I and Type II errors are trivial next to Type III errors, which are working on the wrong problems. There are problems behind the problems. symptoms are often far removed from the causes in organizations. Treating symptoms as problems, and thereby ignoring the underlying causes, usually result in wasted effort and little real progress.

We know this intuitively, but we lack an organized way to allow us to shift through the levels of problems to lock in on the root causes. Following D. Bohm, it is helpful to consider both problems that are at the explicate level, the observables, and problems that are at the implicate level, the hidden problems. The ODS Process considers problems to be like onion rings. The outer rings are the explicate and the hidden inner rings are the implicate problems. However, unlike an onion the levels of organizational problems do not form a strict hierarchy. Problems at any level can create problems at any other level, but problems on the inner rings almost always manifest themselves as problems on the outer rings. Often the best solution of an explicate level problem is the solution of a more fundamental implicate level problem.

The levels of organizational problems employed during the ODS Process. There are three levels to the explicate order problems. At the very outer ring or level 1 are those problems which are visible and explicate. These might include rising costs, product quality defects, too high fixed costs, employee dissatisfaction, etc. The second ring of organizational problems are those due to shifts in the organization' environments. These shifts might include regulatory changes, technological changes, competitive changes, worsening economic conditions, etc. The problems identified in the Level 1, while important, may be due to the shifts in the organization's environments of Level 2. Level 3 consists of those organization problems due to an inadequate organizational design to institutionalize the Main Enabling Processes of change. Thus, an organization design which is, for example, organized about the functions of the organization, may have missed through inattention significant shifts in the organization's environments which, overtime, lead to the observed Level 1 problems.

There are at least four implicate order level problems that may lie beneath the three explicate level problems. Recalling that the ODS Process is based on the theory of the Organizational Hologram, there is Level 4. Level 4 problems are those due to defective operation and/or deployment of the twelve MEPs that foster effective organizational learning. Level 5 consists of those problems due to ineffective organizational learning in response to threats to the organizational commons. An organizational commons is a resource shared by all members of an organization. Ronald J. Oakerson argues that there are four types of attributes or variables that can be used to describe a commons. These include:

(1) the physical attributes of the specific resource or facility and technology used to appropriate its yield; (2) the decision making arrangements that govern relationships among users, as well as relevant others; (3) the mutual choice of strategies and consequent pattern of interaction among decision makers; and (4) outcomes or consequence's.

Levels of organizational problems

A. Organization problems at the explicate level (observable)
   1. Those that are visible and explicit
   2. Those due to shifts in the organization's environments
   3. Those due to inadequate organizational design to institutionalize the Main Enabling Processes (MEPs) of change

B. Organizational problems at the implicate level (hidden)
   4. Those due to defective operation and/or deployment of the Main Enabling Processes (MEPs) that foster effective organizational learning.
   5. Those due to ineffective organizational learning in response to threats to the organizational commons.
   6. Those due to threats to the organizational commons
   7. Those involving defining and regulating the organizational commons

An organization can have many commons such as use of its facilities, capital, technology, etc. Often a major organizational change such as a corporate downsizing results in threats to the organizational commons. Consider the new CEO who gets paid a very large salary and bonus to improve the firm and does so by firing 2,000 workers. This is a threat to the commons of long term employment in the firm and an entitlement to a share of its resources. The organizational commons can be threatened by regulatory change as is happening today in the power industry in the USA or in the financial service industry in the late 970s and 1980s due to deregulation of interest rates and other legislative changes. Threats to the organizational commons evoke anger, and anger often evolves into Level 5 problems. In some cases the problems are so deep that there is the problem of Level 7 involving defining and regulating the organizational commons. Note that there is an unknown Level 8 reflecting the belief that as our knowledge of organizations improve, there may be even deeper problems at the implicate level. The book by Woodward on the decision making at the Clinton White House on economic policy may reflect problems at the deepest level which percolate all the way to Level 1 in consequences.

The state of the science of the levels of organizational problems

There were four interdependent and overlapping sub-communities: (a) the theory developers and testers. (b) the engineers, (c) those developing relevant technologies, and (d) practitioners who apply the science. Sketches the state of the theory, engineering, and deployable technologies according to seven levels of organizational problems described in earlier in table does not describe applications because of their wide variety and specialized nature. It does, however, offer general comments.

Because the origin of the seven levels flows out of the theory of the Organizational Hologram, it stresses the theory, engineering,and deployable technologies more closely associated with this level of development known as process theories and methods for organizational design. Except for Level 2, problems due to shifts in the organization's environments, the general observation is that the higher explicate levels are more developed as a science than the deeper or implicate levels. This reflects the emphasis in the organization sciences in the explicate domain of organizational problems. However, this relative neglect presents an opportunity and, hence, a strong reason to develop the organization sciences at the deeper implicate levels.

As we face rapid and pervasive change, the better developed explicate level science often fails us. The author's own work has steadily worked from Level 1 to Level 5 and working with companies is guiding this work to seriously consider Levels 6 and 7. The notion of the commons is still vague but recent work shows promise. The recent fad of business process re-engineering (BPR), for example, is at the explicate level. BPR employs a deficient concept of process which ignores people, structures, links to other processes, and many of the task resources and their characteristics-in-use. According to some recent reports, this technique creates many organizational problems. In a similar vein, the overemphasis of downsizing companies by firing and laying off people to reduce costs is producing backlash and disappointing outcomes. Both BPR and downsizing create new problems which are the natural consequence of buying into solutions at the explicate level which create or ignore implicate level problems. If the root cause of a problem lies at the implicate level then explicate level solutions are similar to a band-aid and because they ignore the cause, they often, over time, make the problems worse. Not only are such methods classic examples of Type III error, they are also, in most cases, unnecessarily heartless, ethically and morally bankrupt, and ultimately ineffective. These corporate predations destroy the organizational commons which, as their effects erupt at the explicate level. It seems folly to insist on explicate level problem solving to solve problems produced by ineffective prior explicate level analysis. On the other hand, many organizational problems are at the explicate level and can be solved with methods appropriate to this level.

The difficult task in performing an organizational diagnosis is finding the right problem to solve, thereby avoiding Type III errors, in the face of limited understanding in the midst of changing conditions. These difficult and important judgments require multiple sources of information, discipline, patience, and honest analysis.

Multiple sources of information area required

During the ODS Process one obtains many types of information. One does a search for background information about the company; its products, its competitors, its industry, relevant regulations, trade association information, stock ownership, debt, financial information, technology, and trends. It is also a good idea to to gather information about the background and history of its principals. The ODS Process involves interviews with the principals to get a feel for the organization, its opportunities, its problems, and its main strengths and weaknesses. During the administration of the Organizational Diagnostic Survey, respondents ask questions and engage in discussion. One obtains additional information as one answers their questions, discusses concepts, and watches their interactions during the ODS administration.

The Organizational Diagnostic Survey contains many questions whose answers are the law data upon which the judgments are made about the state of the Desired Organizational Characteristics, the Main Enabling Processes, the Holonomic Principles, the Key Implementing Processes, the levels of combined congruency, and the state of organizational knowledge, learning, and intelligence. The end of the Organizational Diagnostic Survey instrument has an open ended comment page in which respondents are encouraged to list, in their opinion and in their own words, the three most important problems facing the organization; the three most important problems facing them as individuals; and the three main strengths of the organization. Furthermore, there is a page of coding information requesting their name, unit, position, and other such data. The willingness of the respondents to share this information provides strong clues about some of the organization's problems. Finally, another type of information is the results from prior administrations of the Organizational Diagnostic Survey. This information is valuable in assessing trends and in evaluating the outcomes of previous interventions.

The task of binding together these streams of data to relate them into some coherent and reasonable explanation is called colligation. Think of colligation as the process of coming up with a story line for understanding the state of the organization. Almost always there are inconsistencies in these streams of data but as the process of colligation evolves, so too does one's understanding of these data. In a sense colligation is akin to a detective game in which eventually the disparate clues yield a clear pattern of meaning. It is this comprehensive understanding that leads to selecting recommended solutions in the form of an intervention.

Selecting an intervention

An intervention to improve the effectiveness of an organization is the outcome of a problem solving process using the DOS Process. Interventions are the proposed solutions to the problems found during the ODS Process. There are three basic modalities of interventions. These are: (a) direct consulting, (b) providing education and training, and (c) developing and/or applying tools for the organization. Most interventions involve at least two of these and often all three. The modality of intervention will, of course, depend upon the results and conclusions of the ODS Process and the needs and capabilities of the client organization.

The organization diagonistic process

Organizational problem solving using the ODS process.

The process of organizational problem solving can be conveniently described in terms of its stages. The process begins with the problem finding stage, goes into the problem formulation stage, thence to the decision making stage, which leads to the implementation stage, and finally into the audit and review stages which provides feedback and set in motion a recycling of the organizational problem solving process. Each stage of the organizational problem solving process can involve, within itself, all of the other stages.

Because of the primacy of avoiding Type III errors, working on the wrong problems, in the ODS Process, the most difficult and most important stage is the organizational problem finding stage. It consists of four steps: 1. Agreeing on the need to the ODS process; 2. Interviewing management team and key personnel; 3. Conducting the ODS survey administration; and 4. Preparing ODS results report documents. The problem formulation stage has two steps; 5. Writing conclusions and recommendations and 6. Presenting results to management team. The decision making stage consists of Steps 7a and 7b which are, selecting recommended solutions o implement, and presenting recommended solutions to participating associates. Step 8, implementing recommended solutions, is the implementation stage. Step (9) follow-up assessment to track progress is the aduit and review stage.

Organizational problem Solving and the level of organizational problems.
The table contains seven levels of organizational problem solving plus an unknown level. The table connects the seven levels of organizational problem solving with the Problem. Finding and Problem Soving Stages. Problem finding begins with the earliest process of reaching an agreement to do the ODS Process. Usually at this step the Management Team is clear about the organizational problems which are visible and explicit. There are often hints about problems due to changes in the Organization's environments and about the organizational design. Rarely does a problem identification occur at the implicate order. It takes time to develop intimacy, trust,and ability to communicate sensitive issues. At the earlier stages the consultant lack tacit knowledge of the organization, he and the management team are strangers to each other and, often converse with mutually strange dialects, usually both sides find it uncomfortable and inconvenient to discuss the possibility of deeper issues until later in the ODS process. With each successive step in the organizational problem solving process, the identification of a problem at each level begins to clarify. By the step in which the ODS Results Report Documents are prepared, problems at Levels 1-5 are generally identified with hints about Levels 6 and 7 which involve the

organizational commons. The preparation of the conclusions and recommendations usually surfaces threats to the organizational commons.

Completes the remainder of problem solving using the ODS Process by looking at the decision making, implementation, and audit and review stages. Note that the Level 7 organizational problems, defining and regulating the organizational commons, does not usually emerge until the implementation is well under way. It is very likely to emerge as an identified problem if the implementation entails the Organizational Audit and Analysis Technology for organizational design. The audit and review stage is essentially a restart of the ODS Process following a period after the implementation stage. The entries in Table depend upon the type of recommended solutions that are selected and the modality of intervention. Education and training interventions are less likely to involve the deeper levels of organizational problem solving than direct consulting. Much depends upon that talent and expertise of the consultant employing the ODS Process and the open-mindedness and cooperation of those in the client organization to even consider the deeper issues. Many young, well trained and intelligent MBAs seem incapable of deeper levels of analysis. Seasoned, senior managers with years of experience are more likely to appreciate the implicate order problems.

ODS forms for organizational learning

There is a family of Organizational Diagnostic

Survey forms. There are two that allow one to calculate organizational knowledge, learning, and I.Q. based on the Organizational Level Learning Model shown in in the figure. The nature of the questions in ODS instruments was explained in Part II of this series. Form G: The Learning Organization has 96 questions requiring 153 responses. Form R: Complete ODS has 175 questions requiring 248 responses. From R, being longer and more complete, yields more information and much more detail than Form G. For example, Form R allows estimation of all 38 congruency conditions while Form G allows only six summary congruency conditions. Form R contains more items per result and so tends to be more reliable. The summary results correlate about 0.97 between Form R and Form G. So, if one just wants the main results, Form G is preferred because it is shorter and easier to administer than Form R and its scores are good predictors.

The responses in either ODS form are separated into a set partition called question sets. Each response is contained in exactly one question set and the set of all question sets includes every question on an ODS Form. There are 38 question sets for Form G and 77 for Form R. The question sets are called Key Implementing Processes. The main difference in the number of question sets is the greater number of congruency conditions allowed in the more complete Form R.

Each question has the properties of a knob because it represents a process. Improving the deployment and execution of these processes increases its score. Each Key Implementing Process (KIP) is a knob of knobs and, hence, a knob. The set partition described earlier has the additional property that each Main Enabling Process (MEP) is the union of a set of KIPs. Some KIPs are involved in more than one MEP. Others involve only one MEP. Consequently, the MEPs, are knobs incorporating the constituent KIP knobs.

There are many interesting interdependencies among the questions, the KIPs, the MEPs, and the Desired Organizational Characteristics (DOCs). The DOCs are not strict unions of a set of KIPs as they may involve only parts of some KIPs and all of others. The properties in the Organizational Level Learning models are also not a set partition of the KIPs. Some KIPs are divided among the key learning processes, the adaptation loops and the linkages.

The MEPs are considered the most important properties of the organizational hologram. The theory of the Organizational Hologram argues that if all MEPs are operating everywhere in an organization, the following results obtain: The organization is simultaneously productive, adaptable, and efficiently adaptable and it has full combined congruency. The next section contains a discussion of how to exploit the structure of the interdependencies to select interventions and to estimate effects.

5 New Model of Organizational Learning

Introduction

'New Model of Organization Learning', describes a new, action oriented approach to organization learning. The new perspective asks readers to consider a different way of thinking about how organizations learn. It describes a model that places simultaneous emphasis on achieving an organization's strategic direction and improving its intelligence. The new approach created by the model focuses on the organization, raher than the individual. It views organizational intellience as an active occurrence maintained through purpose, discipline, and persistence. Learning occurs because the members of the organization are learning as a community are responsible for the development and evolution of four specific kinds of knowledge essential to the organization as a whole. The organization learns as the segments work alone and together, refining and developing the processes supporting th four kinds of organization knowledge.

The new model has several useful properties.

It provides a means to measure the level and evolution of organization knowledge. Further, it can be used to establish a measure of organizational intelligence. It can assess the impact of an intervention on the growth and development of organizational knowledge, and it can identify future interventions that, when enacted, produce incremental improvements in the organization's ability to learn.

The new model is based on the notion on science as a purposeful activity performed by four interdependent communities. These communities include theorists who develop and test theories, engineers who identify the means to solve problems using the theory, those who apply the theory, and tool developers who develop the relevant deployable technologies. The model translates its notion of science as a community to organizations and identifies four interdependent key learning processes. These processes recognize that an organization: (a) is characterized by a theory-in-use, which clarified its strategic direction, (b) develops its own means to implement hte thoery-in-use, (c) serve clients and customers and is involved in applying the theory-in-use and the deployable technologies, and (d) finally, engages in selecting and deploying technologies that support its ability to achieve the other three processes. Each of the processes is indispensable to an organization operating in a competitive market and each affects the other three.

In the new model, the four key learning processes are connected to each other. Theory-in-use is linked to the other learning processes. These links illustrate the driving force and importance of the on-going evolution of an organization's strategic direction. Linkages from the other three key learning processes back to the theory-in-use, and among the other three learning processes themselves, acknowledge the feedback needed to adapt and maintain each of the processes and the organization's strategic direction. Furthermore, each of these four key learning processes has an adaptation loop. The linkags and the adaptation loop for each key learning process illustrate the model's recognition of double loop learning.

Organizational knowledge, learning and intelligence are defined. An organization's knowledge is contained in the four key learning processes. Evolution of the organizational knowledge occurs along the linkages that exist among the boxes and the four adaptation loops. Organizational learning is the evolution of organizational And, finally, effective organizational learning is the purposive, disciplined, and persistent management of the evolution of organizational knowledge: (a) in the face of change (b) while the organization continues to operate.

Development of the Organization Level Learning Model is the use of strong inference. That is, the model developed with a rock solid awareness that scientific theories and models have limitation. They are only as string as their ability to withstand counter examples. Counter examples point out defects which are clues to what needs to be made better. Good theories rarely grow in reactive environments that seek to defend or justify existing concepts or ideas. All theories, eventually, get replaced by something different, by new knowledge.

The search for counter examples led us to create a process performing two simultaneous functions: (a) testing the model, and (b) helping organizations become better at learning. Development of the process recognized the need to, first, create a bridge between the objects in the theory and actual processes and activities in an organization. Second, development of the process recognized organization are complex organisms with many secrets, constraints, and obligations that must be considered. Third, change is rapid and, today, it increases the dynamic complexity facing organizations. Therefore, organizations cannot allow a great amount of time to pass between problem finding and solution implementation. Fourth, if a process is going to help organization in the 'real world', it must recognize facts are not conclusions, conclusions are not recommendations, recommendations, are not proposals, and proposals are not implemented remedies. Real time application of the new model of organizational learning must consider the impact the process and its outcomes create for a client.

The development of the new model of organizational learning illustrates the interplay of theory development, engineering, applications, and deployable technologies. First, there was the initial theory of organizational learning. This led to the development of a survey instrument called the Organizational Diagnostic Survey (ODS) to measure the properties inherent in the model. We designed processes to support application of the survey and worked with clients to apply them. At the same time' a software specialist created software to process this survey data. At each step, progress in any one activity impacted the others. For example, as the theory evolved, this created the requirement to change the survey instrument, which in turn demanded changes in the software, which allowed improvements in the format for reporting the results were presented to the client, and which altered the very processes involved in the work. Our ODS, Form G: The Learning Organization went through four evolutions in nine months.

The process evolved into the Organizational Diagnostic Survey (ODS) process. The ODS process supports the Organizational Level Learning Model and the theory of organizational change of which it is a part. The survey instrument is identified as the Organizational Diagnostic Survey, Form G: The Learning Organization. From G is one of a family of surveys designed to measure an organization's ability to be simultaneously productive, adaptable, and efficiently adaptable. The balance of this article accomplishes two goals. First, it describes the ODS Process as it supports organizational learning. Second, it describes how the organization benefits from the process.

The organizational diagnostic survey process role in organizational learning

Overview of the process and its purpose

The Organizational Diagnostic Survey (ODS) Process recognizes organizations as communities working to accomplish specific goals. The goal, for any one of the organization, is contained in its strategic direction. The organization's ability to sustain and evolve the strategic direction as its environments change, is a reflection of: (a) its ability to learn and (b) the constraints placed on it by its own internal operation. Each organization is unique.

The ODS Process is a holistic strategy. It integrates ODS results with information about the context of the organization, and it creates implementable recommendations to strengthen the organization's ability to learn and improve its performance. It combines the processes of consulting, education, and measurement to assess: (a) how effectively the organization organizes its people, resources, technology, and strategic management processes around the actual work being performed, and (b) how well the linkages that support the evolution of organizational knowledge are working. It simultaneously gives Associates the opportunity to assess their current organization and to visualize it as it could be in the future.

The ODS Process accepts an important desideratum of organizational design. The desideratum acknowledges that the time required to analyze a problem must be less than the time for the problem to change. When the time needed to perform the analysis is excessive, the recommendations may be irrelevant as they may be attempting to correct a problem that no longer exists. Please do not misunderstand. We do not mean to suggest the problem has solved itself. Rather, we are merely recognizing that in today's dynamically complex environments, the problem originally under study may have evolved into another problem during the lengthy analysis.

The components aggregate into eight steps. the steps include: (1) the decision to use the ODS, (2) interviewing the management team and other key personnel, (3) administering the survey using an education-based format, (4) preparing the ODS Results Reports documents, (5) analyzing the results and writing the conclusions and recommendations, (6) presenting the results to the management team, and (7) selecting the implementable recommended solutions and a strategy to support their implementation and presenting the recommended solutions to the Associates who participated in the survey while beginning (8) the implementation of the recommendations, and finally, (9) performing a follow-up assessment to measure the impact of implemented recommendations.

This action oriented process enables the ODS to do more than just 'consider the facts' created by the ODS instrument. It recognizes the role local knowledge plays in developing implementable recommendations. Local knowledge is both explicit and tacit. While the explicit knowledge is readily available, the tacit knowledge is gathered through three sources of interaction with the organization: (a) the interviews with the management team and other key personnel, (b) the administration process,and (c) the open-response section of the survey itself.

As we said in our introduction, the ODS Process represents the engineering application of two theories: (a) the Organizational Level Learning Model, and (b) the theory of organizational change that supports it. It recognizes that a theory about organization is only as useful as its ability to be tested in the world it claims to help. A prime desideratum is the implementation of the recommendations. This desideratum makes us aware of the importance of the knowledge gathered about the actual context of the specific organization we are surveying. That is, while the ODS Process makes assumption about organizations as phenomena, it recognizes that not all organizations are able to respond in exactly the same way. Each organization is confronted by constraints which must be considered when developing implementable recommendations. This does not mean that the constraints are permanent, but it does mean we cannot change them in the short term.

For example, the ability of a telecommunication company's quality assurance group to improve is constrained by two factors impacting its rewards system. First, Associates fall into two major categories: (a) salaried technical professionals and (b) auditors governed by rules associated with membership in a union. The rewards and recognition available to the two groups of Associates are ot based on the same assumptions. Therefore, the organization cannot offer the same incentives to all Associates.

The second factor is created by the larger telecommunications company. The larger company has a rewards program and requires the quality assurance group to conform to the corporate rewards systems. Attempts to institute' local' reward and recognition programs are thwarted. Awareness of these factors impacts how recommendations are written. This is not meant to say that the potential impact of the rewards system is overlooked. Instead, it recognizes the futility of 'beating a horse whose legs are broken'. Until the context allows modification of the constraints, recommendations addressing rewards and recognition systems are counter productive.

Before we begin our discussion of the ODS Process itself, we want to briefly discuss the survey instrument, Form G.. The questions used in Form G represent want we like to call knobs. We call them knobs because each describes a process that can be adjusted much like a rheostat adjusts light in a room or the knob on an old fashioned stereo receiver adjusts the volume. The previous article in this series noted that most surveys of employee attitudes, opinions, and reputational measures contain knobless questions. That is, they lack the ability to clearly define a causal link between the response to a question and the property it is purported to measure. Knobless questions do not specify what needs to be done to alter the 'observed' value assigned to the question.

The questions that make up From G allow us to identify specific action the organization can take to improve the four Key Learning Processes and the linkages that hold them together. Elaborates the Key Learning Processes integral to the Organizational Level Learning Model.

The administration process

The administration, process brings the organization's Associates together to achieve four goals. First, assess the organization. Second, introduce Associates to the terms and concepts that support the survey. Third, as part of follow-up administrations, the process provides a venue to share and clarify Associates' understanding of organizational issues. Fourth, the administration process and the ODS instrument enable Associates to view their organization as it is 'today', and as it could be, if the assessed processes were working throughout the organization.

The opportunity to see the organization as it could be, combined with an introduction to the terms and concepts has two effects: (a) Processes, previously unnamed, are brought to the Associates' attention (e.g. clarifying the assumptions behind the strategic direction can improve Associates' understanding of the organization's actions and improve cooperation with managers). (b) A new basis for conversation is created among participating Associates because they are introduced to thinking 'organizationally' about important issues. For example, if the organization is going to learn as an organization, then the role of a healthy problem solving process is paramount. Problem seeking and problem selection become tied to finding problems whose solutions result in implementable best decisions that are: (a) best overall for the organization and (b) in harmony with its strategic direction.

Finally, the consultant conducting the administration is provided with an additional window into the actual context of the organization through the discussion occurring as part of the administration process. Thus, the administration process itself becomes a valuable source of information and offers opportunities for education and training.

The results reports

There are three Results Reports. These include: (a) the ODS Results Report, (b) the Open Response Comments, and (c) the Manager's Supplement.

The ODS Results Report present the results of the Associates' responses. These results are grouped into four major categories: (a) The Learning Organization, (b) The Desired Organizational, Characteristics, (c) The Main Enabling Processes, and (d) the Organization's Short Term Potential. The Learning Organization results summarize the Associates' assessment across the four key learning processes, the loops effecting them, and the linkages connecting them.

It also contains our measure of organizational intelligence.

The six Desired Organizational Characteristics and twelve Main Enabling Processes present the Associate across: (a) 18 major organizational properties, and (b) the Key Implementing Processes. These properties support the organization's ability to learn and respond to change. The results are presented against a benchmark and a standard of excellence.

Respondents are asked to makes judgments based on a scale ranging from 'Never' to 'Always'. Never equates to 1 and always equates to 5. The interpretation is linked directly to the theory supporting the survey and the Organization Level Learning Model.

Experience with the theory, in over 60 ODS studies, enabled us to set 4.5 as the benchmark for each property. This Benchmark is identified as the World Class Benchmark (WCB). Properties assessed at this level are consistently found throughout the entire organization. Essentially, all Associates recognize these properties as a vital part of the organization's day-to-day operation. For example, managers in an organization that is World Class at 'ensuring compatibility of Associate goals and strategies' consistently counsel and coach Associates to help them align their personal goals and strategies with the organization's strategic direction. Consistency is exhibited through quarterly discussions between the manager and each Associate.

We realized the World Class Benchmark (WCB) represented the 'Ideal'. Therefore, we established a Realistic Standard of Excellence (RSE) at 4.25. The RSE suggests the property is a definite characteristic of the organization, but recognizes that it is not always present for all Associates. The Associates' actual assessment of each property is described along with WCB and RSE. The actual value is compared to the RSE to establish the interval or gap between it and the named property. Illustrate results as reported in terms of two Main Enabling Processes and the Key Implementing Processes that support them. The figure also illustrates how a major property is defined on the report page facing the actual reporting of the results.

The Main Enabling Processes and the Key Implementing Process described are important to key learning processes: Evolution of the Organization's Theory-in-use and Applying the Organizational Means and Deployable Technologies.

Another feature of the analysis in the ODS Results Report is the sensitivity analysis of what would happen to the holonomic properties and organizational learning if one were to intervene to improve any or all of the Key Implementing Processes. We have learned through experience that an intervention intended to improve a KIP from, say, 2.60 to 3.60 is easier than an improvement, from 3.60 to 4.60. As the scores improve, it becomes increasingly difficult to make additional improvements. Our analytical procedure relies on linear programming in which we set preestablished constraints on the maximum improvement possible in the short term. If every KIP were improved from its current value to its maximum, the result is called the Short Term Potential.

For example, suppose an organization has an average score of 3.15 for its Main Enabling Processes. Its Short Term Potential might be 3.95 which is well below the Realistic Standard of Excellence and the World Class Benchmark. Suppose further that the CEO ardently desires to achieve the RSE. The Short Term Potential helps establish more realistic expectations. One of the features of the linear programming model is that it provides the CEO with detailed information about the relative impacts of different interventions. In this example, given the specific circumstances, it might be concluded that even the Short Term Potential is unrealistic. Increasing from 3.15 to 3.60 in a 9 month period might be a tough but realistic performance standard. The output from the linear programming model would pinpoint what combination of improvements in the set of KIPs would be required to achieve this result. Thus, the CEO works with his Associates to develop a strategy of improvements over time with specific accountability for results.

The Short Term Potential, generated by the linear programming model, provides a context-free list of properties and processes that should be adjusted to make improvements in the organization's ability to learn. We shall discuss how this information is used in the section, Recommendations and Conclusions.

The Open Response Report lists Associate responses to three question asked at the end of survey instrument. The three questions are: (a) What do you see as the three most important problems facing your organization? (b) What do you see as the three most important problems facing you as an Associate within the organization? (c) What do you see as the three main strengths of your organization?

The Associates' responses are reviewed and modified, if necessary, to ensure anonymity. One Associate prefaced a response by stating: 'I'm 56 years old and have been with the company for 23 years...', while another began her comment with: 'I am the only woman in my unit...'. Both these comments were generalized in terms of the overall themes of the comment.

After they are recorded the open-response comments are content analyzed in terms of the predominant themes running through them. Then, conclusions are made about the organization based on the comments alone. These conclusions are later integrated into the overall conclusions developed as part of the final report prepared for the client organization.

The third document we create is the manager's Supplement. This Supplement provides a confidential comparison between the senior manager's assessment and the assessment made by the Associates. It allows the manager to determine how 'in touch' he or she is with the Associates.

While some difference is expected, wide gaps indicate deployment problems. A large gap means that the manager's view is inconsistent with the Associates. The manager lacks a well developed knowledge of the day-to-day operation of fundamental business processes influencing the Associates. Out-of-touch managers less effectively cope with the interdependencies impacting their Associates and the organization. The gap creates a disconnect which inhibits the organization's ability to learn. Purpose, persistence, and discipline are missing or are misdirected.

6 The Organisational Assets of the Learning Firm

Introduction

This chapter suggests that the reason for which the notion of organizational capital has played an obscure role in economic theory lies in the way economists utilize static models of the firm. Economists cannot meaningfully differentiate between technological and organizational knowledge because the latter alludes to a dynamic learning process. Also recent contribution by economists have been converging towards representing firms as learning organization, whose capacity to survive and evolve is both enhanced and limited by the codes they use to interpret their environments. These learning codes allow firms to select competencies and choose their boundaries, the essential role of organization capital.

The notion of organizational capital in economics

Organizational capital is an ambiguous concept for economists as they usually subsume organizational knowledge into a firm's production technology by amalgamating the knowledge of 'how-to-do' and 'how-to-organise'. In that context, organizational capital is not particularly relevant because economists model firms as static black boxes utilizing production blueprints to process inputs into outputs. Economists feel the need to call on the factor of production 'management' only when problems arise with the premises of market-based economic theories.

In contrast, the ability to organize and manage production is a central theme in business history, management and the sociology of organizations. In these disciplines, firms possess diverse capabilities creating unequal abilities at exploiting resources, producing commodities and generating profits. Those capabilities encompass production and organizational knowledge assets and jointly determine competitiveness. Chandler and Porter for instance, view firms as becoming competitive through appropriate investments in organizational and technological knowledge, contrasting with traditional economists assuming such knowledge to be exogenous. The increasingly popular suggestion that firms investing early and successfully in innovative managerial structure reap the benefits of scale and scope economics stems from that work. By moving early to construct novel production routines and to establish external distribution networks, firms ca acquire a lasting advantage. Incumbent firms can usually maintain this relative advantageous position on the learning curve until they are confronted with new radical innovations implemented by their competitors. For instance,

Chandler has suggested that the multi-divisional firm was such an organizational innovation, which slowly replaced the traditional functionally departmentalised firms. Enterprises such as Dupont and General Motors which pioneered the M-form, seized significant market shares away from formerly dominating firms by effectively exploiting their improved strategic planning capabilities and incentive structures. Their competitors eventually followed by duplicating the new organizational benchmark, but necessarily lagged behind in adapting the new organizational knowledge to their specific market circumstances. Firms need to invest considerable resources matching their organizational structures and competitive strategies with environmental condition to gain competitive advantage[2]. In that context, 'capabilities' refer to both the technological knowledge and the organisational knowledge help by the firm. Technological competencies and organizational assets are not differentiated as they are conceived to jointly develop and contribute to a firm's competitive position.

Economists neglecting organizational issue can not take comfort by arguing that three have been no antecedents in their discipline. Marshall has argued that 'organization' should be considered a separate factor of production, essential in supporting the growth of knowledge and even initiated the distinction between internal and external organization. But these early insights were to be overlooked as economists elected to analyse industries composed of identical firms, equally capable of transforming inputs into outputs and reduced to making basic price and quantity decisions.

Penrose's economic theory of 'the growth of the firm' constitutes an important exception as she explained the limits to the growth of firms by referring to the difficulties encountered while integrating managerial inputs. In her model, successful firms grow by diversifying into various activities and are constrained mostly by the costs of acquiring and utilising effectively the input 'management'. Her work is unorthodox because it describes differentiated firms acquiring various technological capabilities according to their organisational compatibility. Her very 'Marshallian' contribution stands a part as it can not be reconciled with the conventional 'black box' view of the firm used by neoclassical economists as it puts most of the emphasis on matters of internal organization.

Behavioural economists such as Leibenstein were more successful in drawing the attention of orthodox economists to the notion that business enterprises are rarely homogeneous and can be differentiated on the basis of their differing ability to utilise factors of production. Like Chandler, he argued that large firms capable of coordinating complex sets of resources could gain competitive advantage through their superior ability to manipulate incentives and harness effort. Managers play a crucial role in controlling individual opportunism by designing efficient organizational structures. This is a deceptive proposition because it suggests the existence of an efficiency benchmark applying to organizational assets, like if real-World firms could simply acquire generic organizational knowledge and strive for an organizational efficiency target. In his later work, Leibenstein recognised that the 'relative efficiency of firms vis-a-vis each other' is really the source of competitive advantage but he still failed to describe firms as entities effectively differentiated and evolving unique combinations of technological and organizational capabilities.

The explicit notion that organization is a form of capital has recently emerged at the junction of economics and organizational studies. Tomer utilises the term 'organizational capital', in contrast with capabilities, to describe factors of production interacting with other forms of intangible and intangible capital. He provides a definition.

Investment in organizational capital refers to the using up of resources in order to bring about lasting improvements in productivity and/or worker well-being through changes in the functioning of organizations. Organizational capital could involve 1) changing the formal and informal social relationships and patterns of activity within the enterprise or 2) changing individual attributes important to organizational functioning, or 3) the accumulation of information useful in matching workers with organization situations. Organizational capital is human capital in which the attribute is embodied in either the organizational relationship, particular organization members, the organization's repositories of information, or some combination of the organization.

Thus, organizational capital is embodied in the persons composing the organization and can not be appropriated by an individual. In a static context, the term 'organizational capital' can be misleading because it still seems to imply a distinction between the knowledge of 'how-to-do' and the knowledge of 'how-to-organise' production. This ongoing difficulty is undoubtedly linked with economists' portrayal of technology as a transferable blueprint containing production recipes. Such a representation implies that the firm is only the repository of production knowledge, can modify its technological position simply by acquiring 'how-to-do' information, and can simply add the organizational assets required for implementation. It is still suggesting that firms possess the technological knowledge allowing them to choose least costly mixes of inputs and that they can even substitute management for other inputs. Tomer asserts that firms mix various forms of complementary human and organizational capital which 'add quantitatively and qualitatively to the productive capacity of their internal social and socio-technical relationships'. Although it might be tempting to adopt the idea of a static distinction between transferable production knowledge and less-transferable organizational knowledge, this paper argues that such a distinction can be made meaningful only by shifting to a dynamic model of the firm. It is necessary to distinguish between the organizational assets required for the firm to learn and the technological competencies it incorporates at a point in time. This is the direction taken by various strands of economic thinking about the firm as they converge towards a 'learning perspective', arguably providing a superior framework to interpret the concept of organizational capital.

Organisational capital as market failure

Despite Coase's early appeal, the systematic investigation of the nature of firms and markets has long been overdue. Economists have recently attempted to contrast the performance of real-life firms against that of real-life markets. The 'market failure' approach proposes to contrast the transaction costs associated with alternative forms of economic coordination, usually ranging form arm's length transactions to internal-hierarchical transactions. Firms are selected as superior coordinating institutions when the transaction costs of internal coordination are lower than market transaction costs. Transaction costs are generally construed as contractual costs defined in a broad way[3]. They include the activities required to conceive and follow up agreements over exchanges and to transfer property rights from an individual to another, comprising the resources necessary to:

(a) search for exchange partners (b) negotiate the terms of exchange (c) police the exchange

(d) safeguard the partner's positions in the case of long-term contracts and to remedy the situation if disputes arise.

In the leading theoretical representation of transaction costs, Williamson attempts to safeguard traditional economic analysis by differentiating and adding up production and transaction costs. Transaction costs are system costs traditionally overlooked by economists generally concerned with the ownership of the technological blueprints. Williamson postulates that the institution with the lowest combined costs will be selected by the environment and survive. In a nutshell, if various parties holding small bits of knowledge involved in a technological process must cooperate to produce goods and services, they can coordinate their activities by entering into arm's length contracts or integrate their activities to capitalise on the benefits of planning. The more uncertain and the more specific the nature of the required investments by the cooperating parties, the more likely integrated coordination will be selected over open market contracts. It is particularly economical to establish durable forms of alliance when technological interdependence implies that business units must commit themselves to investments they would not be able to recoup easily or utilise for other purposes. Exchanges inside the firm safeguard the trading parties from having to invest scarce resources to protect themselves against contractual breakdowns with their partners. Accordingly, internal organization is a superior form of coordination to arm's length exchanges when it is costly to align incentives between independent parties. Together, the nature of the technology and the circumstances of specific relationships between firms determine whether a transaction should be executed through market, long-term contract or internal organization. It is important to notice that once again, it is presumed that production and transaction costs can be separated. The diffusion of technological knowledge is independent from the calculation of the transaction costs shaping organizational firms. In the simplest version of the transaction cost approach, technological competencies are exogenously given and firms compete on the basis of their organizational structures. Firms successfully minimising transaction costs are 'naturally selected', and optimal forms of coordination slowly become established. But there is no reason to suppose that technological relationships should be more stable than contractual choices, an essential prerequisite for this model of natural contract selection.

The boundaries of the firm

The question of how firms organise their various competencies can not be separated from that of the selection of those competencies. The idea of the 'boundaries of the firm' refers implicitly to the periphery separating internal from external contracts in given technological environments[4]. A general formulation of the boundaries of the firm requires that the nature of the environment be linked with changes in those boundaries.

Vertical integration

A vertical production chain consists of a sequence of technologically separable stages where the output of a stage becomes the input of the next. Vertical integration is the unified management of any pair of such stages and can be explained by a number of motives. Economists have directed their attention mostly towards the ability of integrated firms to monopolise markets. In contrast, a transaction costs explanation of the boundaries of the firm implies that vertical integration takes place for the sake of economising on those costs which are not incorporated in the would-be exchange price between vertically related production units. Stages of production will gain to be integrated if designing mutually satisfactory contracts for independent transacting parties is likely to be too expensive. The choice of contractual mode is ultimately determined by the characteristics of the product technology. When assets are specifically designed for a transaction and when that transaction involves technologies whose future is uncertain, integration is more likely to be a contending alternative to arm's length exchanges.

The theoretical separation of production knowledge and transaction knowledge is critical to the model,[1] but creates further conceptual difficulties. The transaction costs associated with linking specific stages of production are assumed not to depend on the contractual choices made in the rest of the vertical sequence. This is consistent with Williamson's attempt to make the transaction the basic unit of analysis, which would be justified only if transactional choices did not affect technological choices and production costs. But firms surely expect the choice of boundaries to affect their future capacity to innovate and learn and it seems more sensible to depict transactional and technological decisions as interdependent.

Related to the above issue, we should wonder whether a suitable selection mechanism could discriminate 'efficient' contracts from outmoded ones. Optimal sets of contracts can be selected by competitive forces only if market and technological conditions are sufficiently stable. Even if transactional choices did not affect choices of technology, rapid or volatile technological change could prevent 'optimal contracts' to be selected because optimality can hold only for specific environments. The static transaction cost model is vulnerable because it attempts to safeguard the neoclassical representation of firms as technological blueprints and superimpose an evolutionary process of organizational selection. The knowledge of how-to-produce is assumed homogenous and stable while the knowledge of how-to-organise is diversified, changing and selected through experimentation. This representation of the selection procedure does not allow firms to jointly select competencies and boundaries as the two decisions are artificially split in different time frames.

Economic diversification: lateral integration

Firms also integrate activities which do not fit in a vertical chain of inputs to outputs. They blend activities which are connected through demand and supply technology. Firms incorporate similar activities to exploit economies born from their marketing or technological concentricity. The joint exploitation of activities utilising connected knowledge assets creates synergies or economies of scope. All knowledge-based resources have the property of being shareable and to create potential economic rents in alternative activities. As in Penrose's growth model, firms find it profitable to integrate activities which call on capabilities similar to their own core competencies because they face low integration costs and can acquire competitive advantage over those firms not exploiting the synergies.

The transaction cost explanation extends to the case of lateral integration. When firms perceive that a novel combination of competencies can lead to new market or technological opportunities that could be converted into long-term economic rents, they compare the transaction costs of the integration and market alternatives. The lateral integration of new activities is an attractive solution when it eliminates the risk of costly haggling over the distribution of future profits, especially if the cooperating parties need to make transaction-specific investments. The lateral boundaries of the firm are therefore shaped by entrepreneurial expectations about the evolution of competencies creating profitable synergies. As for vertical linkages, it is problematic to argue that the lateral boundaries of the firm depend on the relative costs of contracting in a given, stable technological environment. A selection process in which technological relationships are assumed stable is even less realistic in the case of lateral integration since changes in boundaries are initiated by the exploration of new technological relationships.

The evolving division of knowledge

Decisions about vertical and lateral boundaries are interdependent, because they both relate to the choice of competencies. They must be integrated in the same strategic decision process, as they are jointly affected by the evolution of technological processes and commodities. Richardson usefully describes the activities of firms as evolving through the connecting principles of complementarity and similarity These two webs of relationships interact and shape the boundaries of firms. A first web is constructed with the spectrum of product technologies found in consumer markets at a point in time. The nature of commodities defines a map of complementary activities to be coordinated in various production processes. Very different competencies are connected because socially-defined commodities require the amalgamation of heterogeneous knowledge assets. As commodities evolve, the linkages between activities shift and the map of competencies to be coordinated changes. For instance, when a commodity such as tourism develops, various activities and services need to be connected. Dissimilar activities which evolved independently such as air transportation, hospitality activities, provision of insurance and financial services for travellers need to be coordinated, possibly to become integrated into packages. As these new linkages are created and some become internalised, others are broke and new firm boundaries emerge.

Similarly, a second net connects activities through process technologies. Knowledge assets are categorised into branch of learning, such as the various fields of scientific and technical knowledge found in education systems. As knowledge grows, the partition are slowly modified to accommodate the changing needs of the research, innovation and diffusion processes. The organization of scientific and applied knowledge is shaped by the institutions which are responsible for the creation and dissemination of knowledge in society. The social division of knowledge evolves slowly and affects the degree of similarity between specific technological competencies. The profitable exploitation of scope economies rests on those evolving categories and the application of given competencies in many contexts or for different products. For instance, a restaurant chain diversifying into hospital catering might extend its competencies to a different commodity because the knowledge assets required in both environments have become increasingly similar. As the technology of fast-food restaurant services has become automated, the once specific competencies evolved to become applicable to the hospital market. The innovative firm improves its competitive position by exploiting those synergies, born from the particular evolution of its knowledge assets and those found in the market.

Richardson describes the environment in which firms operate by blending the neoclassical consumer technology with a Penrosian competencies map. Firms evolve by manoeuvring according to the changing product and process technologies. Those two webs shape the various degrees of relatedness and similarity between production activities and ultimately determine the menu of activities of the firm. To pursue with the example of the restaurant, a fast-food chain might have developed expertise in the management and production of food and beverages which are particularly appropriate for the catering of certain types of hospitals, as the latter as decentralising their activities. That expansion opportunity is the result of innovations in process technologies as well as changes in the nature of the commodity 'health services'. While market forces are playing a larger role in the coordination of health services, the opposite might be happening in the case of some tourism services. As tourism activities become increasingly 'commodified', that same restaurant chain might find it also profitable to coordinate the supply of various travel-related services. There could be pressures to integrate dissimilar services such as motel services, car rental or even tourist attractions because of potential gains from stabilising the product technology. Richardson's framework keeps with the spirit of Marshall in describing the environment of the firm as the interaction of two socially constructed systems. It is now necessary to explore how firms choose how to expand among these evolving opportunities.

Converging theories of the learning firm

Economists have difficulties with the notion of organisational capital because they model static firms with given competencies. They cannot divide organization from technology in a timeless environment without postulating arbitrary causal relationships. Despite this tendency, some economists have attempted to explore the nature of organizational assets in a dynamic context. Three main perspectives are converging.

The evolving firm

A prevailing alternative to the Coasian contractual theory of the firm can be referred to as the 'competence perspective' centred on the evolution of technological and organizational know-how. This approach owes much, to the work of both Marshall and Schumpeter on the ability of capitalist firms to generate new knowledge. Penrose's contribution has already been noted as she viewed the firm as a depository of technological knowledge shaped by attempts to connect similar competencies but constrained by the managerial costs incurred in the process.

Evolutionary economists define firms in terms of the activities they incorporate. Firms hold diversified capabilities stored in routines which re-generate themselves and evolve according to accumulated technological experience and practice.

Competencies incorporate abstract and practical production knowledge, of both an organizational and technological nature. They are jointly selected through the capitalist market system so that 'the heuristic distinction between production and transaction technology upheld in the contractual perspective, loses much of its force and justification'. In that context, organizational capital must play a role linked with the process of acquiring, applying and discarding generic knowledge, rather than being treated as a separate factor of production which firms could substitute to other inputs. The distinction between organizational capital and the knowledge of production blueprints becomes important if the firm is defined as an evolutionary learning engine.

Managing dynamic transaction costs

Many economists have espoused the transaction cost model but few have attempted to combine it with Richardson's insights on the knowledge environment of the firm. Those who took up the challenge had to focus on the transactional difficulties that learning firms encounter when managing simultaneously competencies and boundaries in real time. Firms operating in a Richardsonian environment must anticipate the evolution of the division of knowledge and the changing nature of commodities. The competitiveness of such learning firms depends on their ability to modify and coordinate various ranges of capabilities.

Entrepreneurs face the problem of implementing new technological concepts and maintaining the coordination of various related components. Their central dilemma lies in persuading complementary components to experiment with a new process. Integrated ownership allows for tightly coordinated experimentation when new technologies or new products need to be implemented. Entrepreneurs will consider integrating activities increasingly dissimilar to the core competencies of the firm as long as it is relatively cheaper to learn oneself the new processes than to acquire them in the market. The entrepreneur compares the 'integration production costs' associated with the process of developing new areas of expertise with the 'information transmission costs' arising when a firm needs to contract externally complementary components, themselves requiring specific design changes.

The model is dynamic because firms attempt to gain a technological edge over competitors and face potential delays if much haggling over new designs takes place. They risk losing their competitive edge if they depend on the external provision of complementary inputs. Also, they will invest in costly experimentation and share the costs of learning only if they can trust related producers to withhold new private knowledge assets away from rivals. The related producers hesitate for similar reasons as they cannot evaluate the risks nor potential profits arising from the specific investments they are asked to make. They need to be informed about the totality of the new concept or project, or to trust their partners. Learning therefore creates pressures for close coordination and ultimately suggests an explanation for integration.

This leads to a basic tradeoff between information transmission costs faced while attempting to coordinate arm's-length transactions and the costs of creating that knowledge internally. Parties with different competencies, knowledge and expectations have to be convinced and coordinated to commit resources into new processes or new products whose future benefits and costs they can not evaluate. Systemic innovations arise when large number of complementary activities need to be simultaneously modified while autonomous innovations correspond to radical changes in a single, independent component or stage of production. Firms are more likely to integrate related activities when the nature of commodities is stable and many small modification can improve overall technical efficiency. There will be pressures to disintegrate when demand and competitors are volatile because more diverse autonomous innovations can be generated by independent units. The firm must attempt to anticipate future costs associated with the need to discard competencies when commodities become obsolete. In periods of radical changes, large integrated firms will lack the adaptability of less constrained production units not compelled to safeguard old investments in complementary linkages.

Firms are therefore comparing the costs of

investing in 'internal capabilities' with the costs of arm's length acquisitions in the 'external capabilities' of the market. Production cost advantages are mitigated by relative dynamic transaction costs: 'the costs of persuading, negotiating, coordinating, and teaching outside suppliers'. The relative learning ability of firms and markets determine the boundaries of integration for specific technological systems. In the case of systemic innovations, the internal management of capabilities is a superior form of governance because new concepts need to be implemented across many interdependent stages. On the other hand, autonomous innovations prevail when radical changes in the division of knowledge and the nature of commodities propel the evolution of a technological system. The benefits of decentralised learning are linked to the Marshallian trust that the market process is crucial in generating variations and progress. The market creates the conditions required for high levels of experimentation when its constituents are only loosely connected.

Langlois and Everett argue that the object of vertical integration is not to manage static complexity but to cope with genuine uncertainty and control one's environment. The central advantage of the integrated organization is not simply to allow agents suffering from bounded rationality to assemble large amounts of information about a fully defined environment but to manage uncertainty. As the environment of the firm is unpredictable, the expectations of entrepreneurs about the stability of the 2 connected dimensions of that environment determine the patterns of integration and disintegration found in various industries. When integration is promoted to ensure more stability, existing competencies become more finely tuned but at the cost of greater rigidity. When disintegration occurs, old competencies are destroyed and radical, but local reorganizations occur.

Learning firms and interpretation

Penrose's suggestion that the growth of firms is limited by their ability to coordinate increasingly larger and differentiated mixes of competencies implies that 'management' is an heterogeneous input. Managerial effectiveness depends on the compatibility of individual managerial skills with firms-specific cultures. The productivity of managers increases as they are incorporated in the firm-specific learning process. Firms tend to integrate activities similar to those they already possess because their pre-existing organizational knowledge readily applies to neighbouring areas of expertise.

Firms can supersede arm's length exchanges in organising new knowledge because they create a basis for common interpretations. The role of management is to administer communication codes and to persuade disparate parties to be involved in the development of new and interdependent technological concepts. A firm-specific communication code allows its members to efficiently communicate with each other and prevent rapid diffusion of its distinctive competencies in the environment. Such a tacit mode of communication constitutes a central source of competitive advantage as it limits the transferability of knowledge between firm sand creates sufficient inertia for economic rents to be appropriated. It provides firms with the incentive to innovate by creating sufficient barriers to diffusion.

The organizational capital of learning firms can be given an appropriate interpretation in this dynamic context. Investments in internal and external communication systems play the role of both enhancing experimentation and maintaining stability. The choice of a communication code determines the organizational boundaries of the firm since it limits the number of parties to be linked through this privileged communication system. Codes are best construed as interpretative or cognitive frameworks through which information is not merely transmitted but most importantly interpreted. The notion of a firm's learning codes encompasses both the roles of interpretation and communication. It encapsulates the concept of organizational capital because it refers to the resources retained for the internal transmission and construction of an organization's mindset. This is the principal advantage of internal organization over markets when the environment is evolving smoothly and no radical changes in interpretations are required. Learning codes embody the theories and models through which interpretations of the environment are constructed and through which decisions are taken. Whether they are incorporated in formal rules and procedures or whether they result from the development of informal organizational routines, learning codes solve the problem of maintaining a sufficient distance between the firm and its environment. Incentives to innovate are therefore closely linked with the ability to manage learning codes because a firm's production potential can not be simply stolen or copied by other parties. This indirectly provides a rationale for vertical integration.

But investments in learning codes are imperfectly reversible and limit the growth of firms. The advantages they create in limiting entry are counterbalanced by the barriers to exit they impose on inflexible incumbents, an other theme found in Penrose's limit to growth. Interpretations can be modified only slowly and limit the ability to acquire and discard competencies. The rigidity of learning codes becomes a serious problem as the number of participants and activities within the firm's organizational boundaries increases. The costs of updating the code can become so prohibitive that a total re-structuration of the organizational routines and culture become necessary. Interpretation systems are constructed specifically to avoid investing in revisions and to economise on thinking. Their value lies in their capacity to reduce noise in environments saturated by informational overloads and uncertainty. Efficient interpretations must come at the price of limiting the capacity to generate new avenues for learning. They ultimately lock firms into learning paths which they can not easily escape.

Drastic revolutions in interpretations systems sometimes occur when old views of the World do not perform well and need to be replaced. Large numbers of events conflicting with established theories can trigger such paradigmatic shifts. When learning codes frequently lead to disappointing results, incumbent firms can try to discard the evidence. At the risk of facing a worse crisis later, they might attempt to maintain their short-term internal stability by ignoring signals calling for a revision of their codes. They might also attempt to directly stabilise their environment by taking active steps to influence its future shape. Alternatively they can decide to update major parts of their codes and interpretations, at the risk of facing costly disruptions due to internal inconsistencies. A major revolution requiring a complete alteration of the central constructs of a firm is paramount to the creation of a new firm, as its organizational capital is totally transformed. If such a reconstruction is indeed possible, large amounts of resources have to be invested in the negotiation of new interpretations, without the benefit of experience. This is why firms resist transforming radically the interpretations they have evolved over long periods of time.

A dynamic theory of learning codes forces economists to abandon static and deterministic models in which firms maximise an objective variable, such as profits or sales. Instead, firms attempt to maintain their integrity and safeguard their coherence by choosing among a number of learning and organizational strategies. They slowly accumulate and adjust their organizational capital to secure appropriate competencies as their environment is changing. The competitive process plays an indirect but essential role in selecting those firms which have developed, thanks to both design ability and chance, successful learning codes. Because they have evolved competencies appropriate for specific market environments, firms are at risk of seeing many of their competencies suddenly becoming redundant if the nature of that environment changes suddenly. The latter occurrence would add up to a 'technological catastrophe' if the core competencies of the firm are affected. A balanced mix of competencies allows a firm to maintain a competencies position without exposing it to extreme risks if a downturn in its core business occurs. This is the source of an important strategic tradeoff between the desire to exploit synergies leading to accelerated growth and the need to maintain safeguards against unilateral disasters.

Learning strategies as organisational capital: an economic tradeoff

When they invest in learning codes, firms commit themselves to a type of organizational capital, which shape their menu of competencies and their boundaries. Those codes determine the number and types of actors to be connected though common interpretations, hence the boundaries of the firm.

Two dimensions of the code are particularly relevant in shaping the competencies of the firm. The breadth of a learning code refers to the diversity of experiences disseminated in a specific communication network and varies with the degree of dissimilarity between the actors connected through that code. A code is 'broad' if it allows the coordination of communicating parties operating with disparate constructs. Conversely, a 'narrow' code is sufficient to coordinate a team of homogeneous individuals. The second important dimension of a code is its depth or intensity, referring to its ability to efficiently convey complex messages in real time. A 'deep or intense' code allows rich and highly idiosyncratic information flows to be circulated while a 'superficial' code carries little precision.

These stylised attributes of communication codes convey important insights about the technological compromises involved in learning. Both broad and intense codes are costly when compared to narrow or superficial ones. The development of a deep code implies the construction of a highly specialised, rich and jargon-like language. As in Penrose's account, managerial costs include the training and selection of suitable candidates to become team members, and those costs are greater when a more specialised language is required for intensive experimentation. The advantage of such a costly investment is that it maintains a large number of high quality interactions necessary for fast communication and autonomous learning.

Implementing a broad learning code to link heterogeneous agents also involves a larger cost than would be otherwise required. The sheer complexity of connecting different constructs to establish coherent interpretations consumes much resources. Developing a uniform corporate culture might be desirable but comes at the costs of continuous haggling, negotiating and interacting between heterogeneous individuals.

A rudimentary economic tradeoff between breadth and depth characterises the learning code technology and leads to economies of specialisation. In a given technological system, learning units specialising in either broad or deep codes will be competitive because they will exploit those learning economies. This basic tradeoff based on the technology of learning codes carries important insights for the management of firm boundaries and competencies. Firms integrate or disintegrate activities according to the type of code they invest in.

For instance, enterprises can gain a competitive edge by expanding their competencies across related activities and capitalising on broad codes to link vertical stages of production. There are limits to that process as business units can not let their codes become too diluted, since decreasing returns would reduce their relative advantage over the market. Moreover a superficial code ceases operating as barrier to diffusion so that ideas generated by a highly vertically integrated firm could be appropriated by competitors, unless public and private institutional devices are created to protect proprietary knowledge. Alternatively, learning units can specialise in deep codes to gain competitive advantage. They would also eventually face decreasing returns from excessive depth as the enhanced experimentation made possible by the richer communication flows would lead to excessively peculiar and idiosyncratic ideas. This results in products and technological processes which can not easily be commercialised because of their limited capacity to fit into established technological and social modes. Many radical innovations are generated but not implemented because of a mismatch between the firm's ability to innovate and to promote new concepts.

Business units will therefore tend to specialise in one type of code and accumulate competencies accordingly, by favouring vertical or lateral linkages. They are constrained to a type of organizational capital as they face decreasing returns in either types of learning relative to the market. Once their organizational capital matches their menu of competencies, business units are locked-in a learning strategy. Flexibility is topical as corporations have come to consider the possibility of managing various codes, some broad and some intense. Organisational flexibility refer to the formation of internal boundaries within a firm allowing the management of different business unit within a single corporate entity. Such organizational designs have indeed inspired economic theories of internal organization compatible with the learning code explanation proposed in this chapter.

For instance, the multi-divisional firm described by Chandler and analysed by Williamson has been rationalised by its ability to divide strategic decision-making from routine operations. The multi-divisional form can be interpreted as an attempt to manage various levels of depth and breadth in different parts of the firm. Upper-management synergies can be exploited without burdening basic operations with overwhelmingly sophisticated codes. The division of the corporation along product lines aims at generating sufficiently broad codes to maintain product-based innovations in each product division. Highly radical innovations requiring deep codes are managed separately in centralised strategic and R&D divisions. The topical Japanese firm, on the other hand are characterised by their efficient utilisation of on-the-spot knowledge for rapid problem-solving. Local coordination supplants technocratic control because small operating units manage their own codes. Working teams inside the firm are expected to develop their own interpretations and adapt their operations locally.

Both the multi-divisional structure and the Japanese model attempt to marry depth and breadth by loosely coupling learning codes. In the former case, 'depth' is managed centrally at the strategic planning level while broad codes are used in the competing divisions coordinating the diverse aspects of product development. In the Japanese firm model, 'depth' is managed locally by evolving semiautonomous teams, while 'breadth' is managed centrally as large amounts of resources are invested in building organisational loyalty to maintain coherence between teams. Because Japanese firms invest in the management of broad learning codes centrally, they can afford to trust teams innovating and specialising locally. Modern American corporations however, maintain their coherence by separating their strategic planning capabilities away from the competing product lines. This explains why successful Japanese manufacturers have been closely associated with process innovations where teams have evolved deep and local codes fitting well within stable product configurations while American manufacturers have been described as having a comparative advantage in the implementation of highly uncertain concepts.

Conclusion: organisational capital between flexibility and coherence

This paper argues that the notion of organizational capital is likely to remain problematic for economists, unless they shift to a dynamic theory of the firm based on the ability to learn. It calls on the Marshallian insights of Penrose and Richardson to link the learning strategies of firms with their capacity to coordinate rent-generating competencies. It also shows that economists attempting to explain the force shaping the boundaries of the firm are converging towards such a 'learning firm' perspective.

I interpret organizational capital as a firm's investment in a learning strategy and argue that the technology of learning explains the boundaries of corporations. Firms invest in learning codes to make sense of their environment and generate novel interpretations. The problem with these interpretations is that they are imperfectly reversible and can make organizations ill-adapted to volatile change in their environments, forcing business units to specialise in a type of organizational capital. They will invest in a small number of similar activities or will attempt to successfully exploit the coordination of dissimilar but related activities. As they increase their mastery of a type of learning strategy, production units loose the ability to shift to the other type. There is an ongoing strain within organizations between the desire to maintain coherent learning code by specialising in a single form of organizational capital, and the need for flexibility. The latter can be achieved by dividing firms in parts, each using different types of codes. Managing internal insulating barriers to keep some interpretations apart is a source of genuine flexibility and can be incorporated in the organizational assets of the firm. Indeed, organizational innovations such as the multi-divisional form and the Japanese-organic model can be interpreted as such flexibility-enhancing strategies.

But preserving loose couplings within an organization does not come without costs as it may threaten organizational coherence. If pushed too far, system decomposability can lead to 'organizational schizophrenia' where extreme flexibility induces large numbers of inconsistent decisions within the organization. Loasby points at the trade-off between adaptability and coherence:

> 'Indeed, the redrawing of organizational boundaries is usually intended to invalidate old constructs which were through to be leading to decisions that are now judged to the undesirable when assessed from some higher viewpoint. Restructuring is intended to improve policy through the use of more appropriate theories. ... Partial insulation may allow the development of simpler constructs within each field of interest, making management more effective within those limits. The art of organizational design requires the creation of such insulating barriers where they will facilitate good and low-cost local decision-making, while maintaining a sufficient communality of framework to ensure that the outcomes of local decisions are not disastrous - for example, that products designed to replace the existing range are not totally outside the manufacturing competence of the existing equipment and work force'.

A related danger is to attempt to shelter the firm's codes and competencies too strictly and no underestimate the benefits of market exchanges on learning. Combined flexibility and reciprocity are essential to generate new ideas, and firms must be ready to allow learning partners to access their codes to a certain extent. The simplistic dichotomy between internal and external learning strategies looses some of its relevance as the Marshallian concept of external organization re-emerges under the heading of networks. Learning alliances transcending firm boundaries are important because they shift the location of organizational capital outside the firm and raise important issues regarding the competitiveness and learning capacity of whole industrial systems.

7 International Technology Transfer, Intercultural Communication

Introduction

It is widely accepted that technology transfer from government or university researchers to commercial users is fraught with difficulty. Among the difficulties, problems of communicating stand alongside problems associated with financing, licensing, national security and so on. In an early study completed at the Massachusetts Institute of Technology the importance of 'technological gatekeepers' in R&D information flows and technology transfer was identified. This MIT study also stressed the importance of interactions with organizational colleagues, of interconnectedness, and physical proximity for information and technology flows. When, as is increasingly now the case, technology transfer takes place across national boundaries, the process, which is difficult even within a national/sociocultural unit, becomes a very complex one. The common technology transfer communication problem of communicating between the diverse technocultures of the laboratory and the market is made more complex by distances involved and the additional layer of sensitivities required for effective communication at the intercultural/international level.

Communication in international technology transfer is now recognised as too important, and too complex, to be left to chance. The trend is too seek to influence the process and to manage it for success. Elsewhere, we have taken a boundary spanning approach to demonstrate how technological gatekeepers acting as 'brokers', matchmakers', go-betweens' or 'linkage champions' can bring together key people from both sides, or technocultures, in the cause of transferring technology. This process, we have argued, is one of the newer dimensions of managing corporate communication. It is a process that has been enhanced and facilitated by the rapid growth of strategic alliances in many industries including the aerospace and telecommunications industries we have chosen to illustrate our argument.

Technology transfer issues

Clearly available evidence suggests that technology transfer plays a central role in long-term economic growth. It is not surprising, then, that the study of international technology transfer has resulted in an ever growing large body of research over the last two or three decades. Certainly, there is an ongoing attempt to assess the validity of the phrase 'technology transfer' and the very nature of the process, ranging from clear 'transfer' to the concept of 'sale' to the more complex issue of 'transferring know-how'. Zhao and Reisman argue for meta research on technology transfer, calling for a need to move across taxonomies proposed by and for specific disciplines. Yet, in spite of the spate of research work in the field, very little has focused on intercultural or communication concerns as key issues affecting effective 'transfer' per se.

There are, however, a myriad of other variables considered. For example, Korson and Vaishnavi argue that current management processes are often unproductive in the management of technology transfer in emerging software technologies. Attempts to collaborate on technology transfer by large organizations are often damaged by territorial problems and constant corporate restructuring. They argue that for such transfers there should be an independent legal entity, a lean and small organization that is actually sponsored by multiple organizations, and that there should be a balance of power between the organization's leadership and the corporate sponsors.

Technology transfer suffers not only from difficulties in bridging cultural differences but also relates to difference in expectations relating to roles and goals in diverse organizations. It is increasingly recognised that 'ultimately, technology transfer is less a task to be accomplished than a set of relationships to be nurtured'. In improving technology transfer strategies it is clear that goals and needs differ in the work environment. This requires not only analysis of culturally different needs profiles and how these interact but a real recognition that management processes that work well in one country are not necessarily transferable to other cultures. Moreover, communication across corporate cultures Iisoften no easy matter, and communication difficulties, both at micro and macro levels, can act to significantly hinder technology transfer.

Technocultural difference

Technocultures are sub-cultures distinguished by their technologies and their attitudes to technology. They develop from the web of interactions among technologies and approaches to workforce skill formation, work organisation and practices. They are complex and, like other dimensions of culture, they vary widely. Like other sub-culture of the 1990s, they can change rapidly.

Micro-level researcher and commercial user technocultures, with their idiosyncratic language and coding systems and differences between academic/research and commercial cultures, are in marked contrast. Their differences must be recognised as a potential barrier to the communication essential in technology transfer. Macro-level technocultures, though perhaps less obvious, may act as a further key impediment to communication and technology transfer.

Ford has drawn attention, for example, to the differences between the technocultures of Germany and English speaking nations and their consequences for international technology transfer. Whereas German technocultures emphasise worker flexibility and thus allow individual involvement in absorption, application and further development of new technologies, the labour forces of English speaking nations are usually characterised by strong demarcations that permit very little integration between researchers and skilled workers. The same writer goes on to argue that Australian technocultures emerged from nineteenth century British concepts of technology, hierarchical organizations, 'trade unions' and conflictual relations overlaid by twentieth century American concepts of mass production, fragmentation of work, authoritarian control and narrow-skilling of workers. According to Ford, this technoculture, protected as it was by isolation and tariffs, encouraged development of complacent, non-adaptive, rigid and inwardly focused management and unions. Australian technocultures have not been conducive to technology transfer. They have tended not to encourage individuals to be pro-active in intercultural communication aimed to assist the transfer of technology.

Severe problems for smooth technology transfer arise when, as often is the case, there are market differences between donor and recipient technocultures. New technologies being transferred to Australia from Germany or Japan have often been developed, and are often transferred, on the assumption they will be used by multiskilled workers not bound by the traditional Australian system of demarcation. When this happens there can be extreme difficulty in adopting or implementing what will be perceived to be unworkable or alien technologies so that technology transfer will be impeded and delayed.

Clearly, the emerging evidence in much of the organizational literature reinforces what has long been suspected - that international business negotiations and alliances are significantly influenced and complicate by cultural variations which influence personal communication. These include attitudes to relationships, to markets, to management styles, business practices, negotiation behaviours, and also value and ethics conflicts.

Yet, while undeniably many are becomin sensitised to culture as a critical factor affecting management practices and strategies, technology transfer per se is an area that has received little attention in the growing research and literature on intercultural business communication. The influence of cognitive frames, differing across cultures, as a basis for communication processes in technology transfer has received virtually no attention in the technology domain.

A recent case study investigated the influence of perceptions of transnational corporate executives on technology transfer into Mexico. The study argued that such perceptions affected the transfer of technology in very specific ways and points to the need to understand such culture variables in assessing the process of technology transfer. Parke also focused on culture in terms of organizational learning and global strategic alliances. He highlighted the dangers of ethnocentric arrogance, the way national contexts hamper effective collaboration, and the importance of differences in GSA corporate cultures. These studies point to the increasing significance of the links between cultural sensitivity, Intercultural communication and technology transfer, and the importance of 'people connections' in making technology transfer happen.

Strategic alliances and intercultural corporate communication

In the climate of recession, layoffs, mergers and the like, efforts to rationalise business operations and improve overall organizational effectiveness have raised the profile of strategic alliances. The increasing speed and dynamism of technological change has spurred the process along and, for many, strategic alliances appear as the latest hope for survival and prosperity in the highly competitive 1990s. The immediate benefits of capital pooling along with mutually beneficial goals in R&D and new market penetration are obvious and quickly embraced. What is not so obvious however, is the way in which strategic alliances open up opportunities for contact between individuals in ways not possible in the previous environment in which alliances did not exist. New networks formed and encouraged by strategic alliances open up fresh opportunities for technology-transferring communication activity. Macro-level organizational restructuring involving strategic alliances permits communication for technology transfer at the level of organizational learning. At the same time, this macro-level organizational restructuring rearranges and expands micro-level or personal communication networks, and brings into contact people who can effect the transfer of technology. The case studies included in this article illustrate macro and micro-level inter-organizational learning and how it has facilitated Australia's participation in the international aerospace and telecommunications industries.

Personal networks, particularly those created or expanded when strategic alliances are formed, have been shown to have played an important part in technology transfer. For example, Rogers and Valente have shown that personal networks facilitated the informal collaboration needed for innovation and creation of spin-off companies in Silicon Valley. In recent times, networks and strategic alliances among corporations, research institutes and universities have received increasing attention as devices formed to help achieve the economies of scale and critical mass necessary to participate in the global marketplace dominated by large multinational corporations. Formed for those reasons, international networks and strategic alliances such as those involving Australian participation in the aerospace and telecommunications industries then also assist the intercultural communication necessary to facilitate international technology transfer. This personal communication dimension of international networks and strategic alliances holds considerable power for enhancing international technology transfer.

While there is no question that it is people who effect information flows and technology transfer, the further question arises whether direct personal contact is essential for this to occur. The answer to this question is that while electronic communication such as EDI, email and the transfer of CAD data now allow instantaneous information transfer between remote locations, organizations that are successful in international technology transfer use periods of personal exchange to allow staff to form personal and trusting relationships.

As it is people who do the communicating in international technology transfer, it is of central importance that attempts to improve the process take on a human resource development perspective. Discussions about the association between technology transfer and human resource development often focus upon the need for general and specific training and education in receptor technocultures or nations to ensure effective take-up of a transferred technology. One such account indicates three stages: recruitment and training of local workers to master and implement the technology; advancement of these workers, after further training, to replace expatriates; and the turnover of trained managerial staff to commence new enterprises and diffuse the transferred technology. Clearly, the interactions that occur in all of these stages may enhance communication and the international technology transfer process.

At another level, however, it is also important to focus upon a neglected area of human resource development essential in promoting technology transfer. Where international transfer is being contemplated, the boundary-spanners, brokers, matchmakers, go-betweens or linkage champions need to move comfortably between at least two national cultures as well as between researchers and the commercial marketplace. While many of the specialists operating in these roles may have had experience in the latter, few have had the experience to move comfortably between the cultures of the nations involved and in ways that promote the sensitivity and communication fundamental to effective technology transfer. Those actively involved in technology transfer across international boundaries will often require education and development in intercultural communication.

This latter view of human resource development, which expects competence in intercultural communication, begs the question of how that competence is to be attained? While it is well accepted that cultural sensitivity is the foundation of effective intercultural communication, what is not clear is how cultural sensitivity is best enhanced and then used in ways that improve communication between cultural/national groups. Intercultural communication 'training' based on Edward Hall's notion of the anthropology of manners—ways, customs, practice and etiquette - has influenced the field of intercultural communication through to the present and remains its most dominant influence.

The manners approach is most clearly manifest in do's and don'ts quick-fix tips lists presented in short Courses, books, magazines, audiotapes and, more recently, computer software packages. While it appeals because it promises instant results, the manners approach to intercultural communication is superficial; stops short in its capacity to assist people to understand 'frames of reference' necessary to interpret cultures; focuses to excess upon overt, observable behaviours; is paternalistic and, at worst, racist.

Colonial anthropology was the basis of the manners approach to intercultural communication. Post-colonial anthropology, and the new field of intercommunal studies, with their emphasis upon communal and national identities rather than personal behaviour catalogues, are fast becoming the basis of a new approach to intercultural communication which can be thought of in terms of an anthropology of identity. The value of thinking in terms of identities comes from the capacity of the approach, via deeper analysis and 'thick descriptions', to provide a more robust basis for developing the frames of reference necessary to understand and interpret culture and to enhance cultural sensitivity. The identities approach encourages thinking in terms of Australianness, Chineseness, Germanness and so on; in terms of a 'people', including that people's diaspora; in terms of 'cultural ecology', as in Thompson's account of the ascendancy of a Pacific cultural ecology over the previously dominant Atlantic social ecology; and in terms of broad cultures such as those identified by Huntington as North American Western and European Western, Confucian, Japanese, Islamic, Hindu, Slavic-Orthodox, Latin American and African, and for which religion is often central to understanding identity. This richer approach to cultural sensitivity and improved intercultural communication via identities, while more rewarding, must be recognised as more rigorous and time consuming and requiring a major effort at 'culture learning'. And amongst other things, this culture learning, to be worthwhile, needs to develop the capacity to deal with the challenge of rapidly changing communal and cultural identities, including those of the strategic alliance itself and its members. This is important given that organizational structures of strategic alliances enhance opportunities for intercultural communication.

Australian aerospace industry

The Australian aerospace industry is heavily reliant upon international technology transfer. Although the first aircraft designed and built in Australia flew in 1909, and there have been several successful aircraft development projects since that time, the industry is small and forms only a tiny part of what has become one of the world's first truly globalised industries. In a country which today has a population of only 17 million, which is distant from American, European and newer Asian aerospace industry concentrations, and which has been distant from this century's theatres of war, the Australian industry has always faced the difficulty of diseconomies of scale. The industry has relied heavily on a defence workload supplemented by maintenance work for domestic and international carriers. Heavy reliance upon defence workload has produced an industry characterised by cycles of activity and inactivity, and one dependent upon receipt of technology from overseas. The present downturn in defence work, the world recession and associated substantial passenger and freight carriage reductions, and the unwillingness of money strapped Australian governments to continue the earlier practice of generous industry off-sets, have forced industry players to urgently seek international niche markets as a matter of survival. Adapting quickly to meet the needs of these international niche markets has involved the industry in a further intense period of technology acquisition through international technology transfer.

Hawker de Havilland is Australia's largest aerospace company. In addition to its significant airframe work, it is the country's largest aero engine company, with that work primarily involving assembly and maintenance. HDH is a niche participant in international programs with Boeing, McDonnell Douglas, British AeroSpace and Northrop. Aerospace Technologies of Australia currently fully owned by the Australian government, is the second major airframe company. Its international niche work involves Boeing, British Aerospace and Aerospatiale. When ASTA's responsibility for assembly of F/A 18 fighters for the RAAF was completed in 1990 it diversified into maintenance and modification of Boeing 747s. Qantas, Ansett Airlines and Australian Airlines are involved with in-house maintenance work, with Qantas also contracting maintenance work for the RAAF and international carriers. AWA Defence Industries dominates the avionics and defence electronics areas of the industry, areas shared with British Aerospace Australia. Several subsidiaries of overseas companies share Australian-based aircraft systems work. These include BTR Aerospace, Lucas Aerospace and Normalair Garrett.

HDH's experience in managing technology transfer demonstrates a number of important aspects of the international technology transfer process, including the work of linkage champions and the communication spin-offs from the strategic alliances formed in response to the development of niche marketing. As HDH suffered from the decline of its specialised airframe programs, it developed significant niche marketing programs with primes such as Being, McDonnell Douglas and British Aerospace, for whom it now specialises in advanced composite materials, computer controlled component machining and precision metal structures.

The motivation for technology transfer at HDH has been closely associated with the company's move to internationalisation as a matter of survival. When the guaranteed government directed flow of defence work that kept HDH in business throughout the second World War and to the early 1970s ceased, the company was left with almost no aerospace load. It then faced the task of quickly achieving international levels of technology competence and productivity. In achieving its objectives in this area, HDH unashamedly engaged in imitation and in a period of copying and producing overseas designs under licence. For example, Boeing equipment purchased as surplus in the United States was shipped to Australia and used in a direct technology transfer process that ensured production processes corresponded with international, world best practice, originals.

Again, very direct communication processes were involved in the acquisition of technology which introduced composite bonding, metal bonding and automatic riveting to Australia. HDH sent Australian tradesman to Boeing's Seattle facility to work alongside their American production-line counterparts to learn production techniques. Linkers and linkage champions, who were engineering and commercial managers at HDH and Boeing, orchestrated the international boundary spanning activities that led to the success of these transfer efforts. In this regard, it is instructive to note that a characteristic of the Australian aerospace industry is that its senior commercial management personnel are quite often also qualified aeronautical engineers. Thus, boundary-spanning across the technical/commercial technocultures, and in this instance across national cultures, is facilitated by personal contact.

A further characteristic of the global aerospace industry is the extent of international networking and strategic alliances. Aerospace industry alliances extend from 'hands-off' agreements, to manufacturer under licence, to more wide ranging alliances involving long-term planning collaborative R&D, and joint manufacture. Because of its relative isolation in Australia and its dependence on international know-how, HDH has been active in international networking for nearly half a century and this networking has been the basis of participation in strategic alliances now seen as critical for success as a player in the global industry. For example, HDH is now the sole world source for Boeing 747 wing leading edge flap systems, for Boeing 737 ailerons and Boeing 757 wing ribs. It is also a major supplier of wing ribs and carbon fibre landing gear doors for the Airbus family of airliners, and it supplies McDonnell Douglas with metal elevator tail sections for DC9/MD80 airliners. The international strategic alliance business structure has provided the communication framework for the technology transfer necessary to develop this niche manufacturing activity.

A very clear illustration of how communication works to assist international technology transfer within the framework of a strategic alliance is provided by HDH's collaboration with the McDonnell Douglas MDX helicopter program. The MDX light/medium civil military helicopter program involved developing and manufacturing the airframe at Bankstown in

Sydney with McDonnell Douglas developing the aircraft's systems integration in the United States, with HDH contributing 20 per cent of the investment capital. As airframes interface with aircraft systems, every change in one, however small, affects the other. In this situation, where constant interaction about aeronautical engineering technology within the alliance is necessary, communication has been carefully managed to assist international technology transfer. The fundamental communication problem in the helicopter's 1992 design phase was ensuring that aeronautical engineers on both sides of the Pacific working on separate but inter-facing systems were working from a current, and common, date base. This date base was being altered at the margins on numerous occasions each day. The communication-for-transfer solution was found by both firms using the Unigraphics II computer aided design system which allowed daily information transfer between the HDH and the McDonnell Douglas data bases so that no designer worked from a data base more than twelve hours old.

While the MDX design work also illustrates almost simultaneous two-way technology transfer on an international electronic data base, most of the international transfer referred to in this summary account of the Australian aerospace industry has been transfer acquisition by Australian firms. And, again as in this illustration, the international communication involved has been between like cultures. For those involved in the Australian aerospace industry, both of these characteristics of the process of technology transfer are changing. Australia is seeking to become a source of aerospace technology for outward transfer, and the significant growth of the aerospace industry in Asia means that quite different national cultures are coming to be involved in a aerospace technology transfer.

The former change has involved a major restructure and expansion of Australia's aerospace research effort. This has involved expanded research facilities in a number of Australian universities and the establishment of a Cooperative Research Centre known as the Aerospace Structures Research Centre. The centre involves HDH, ASTA, the Aeronautical research Laboratories, The Royal Melbourne Institute of Technology, Monash University and the Universities of Sydney and New South Wales. This multi-institutional, multi-sector research centre, founded on the government's 'clever country' initiatives of 1990, is focusing research in the areas of composite materials and structures. The centre is structured to support and expand communication links between researchers and users including those who are international project partners of centre members. Elsewhere in Australia a number of space Industry Development Centres, co-ordinated by the Australian Space Office, have been established in universities to conduct research to develop technologies to be marketed internationally, or transferred to world markets. Further, the recent breakthrough in scramjet technology at the University of Queensland has enormous potential for transfer to the international marketplace. The ten-year scramjet development project about to begin there will occur during a period of major change in the international/intercultural dimension of technology transfer. It, along with the range of other aerospace technologies under development in Australia, will be transferred internationally, often to potential market places in cultures very different from the North American/ European western cultures which have, in the past, dominated the aerospace industry.

Aerospace technology transfer to Asian nations and cultures will add another dimension of complexity to an already complex process. Certainly, it will not proceed effectively if those involved are so unaware of the role of cultural sensitivity in communication and negotiation as to ignore it or rely upon quick-fix tip lists. These new, Asia-involved, linkage champions will need to work carefully in terms of national identity and to understand the subtleties of difference in negotiating styles, business etiquette and practices, legal procedures and so on in the context of national/cultural histories; political, legal and social systems; and religions - in terms of identities. This is no small challenge and one, in human resource development terms, requiring considerable change in organizations which - along with the other challenges they face - must become Asia-literate.

Australian telecommunications industry

Australian telecommunications is currently undergoing the most rapid and perhaps the most significant change that has taken place in its history, while the Australian industry is presently absorbing major structural change in an intensely competitive environment. The nature of the industry is changing substantially and Australian industry and government must be geared to react and capitalise on these changes to capture the benefits. The real alliance between government and industry needs development, including the communication dimensions of the relationship. The physiology, and even the very existence of present carriers and suppliers, will increasingly be shaped by moves from monopoly to multi-carriers, the emergence and application of new equipment and services, the role of the global carriers, the entry and growth of multiple service providers and the emergence of a more demanding and adoptive client base.

Not surprisingly, then, there is a new imperative to innovate, to increase the range and speed of introduction of new services and to compete for domestic and international customers which is substantially changing the nature of the relationship between carriers, suppliers 8and customers.

While, in international terms, the Australian industry is small in comparison to its major developed country competition it is comprehensive and technology-rich in both its product range and the quality of its skills and output. It is also highly capital intensive with substantial investment in a number of world class plants, in people and training, in research and development and in production. The industry is endeavouring to increase its international status in terms of benchmaking and developing world best practice standards of equipment and performance.

Again, not surprisingly, many public statements and comments on the current performance of the industry contain the message that the Australian industry is strong and confident, with total output measured in billions of dollars and that it is experiencing strong growth in domestic value added, technological capacity and export performance. Indeed, in many ways the structural change in this industry is a model for dramatic and successful micro-economic reform.

Yet much still needs to be done to consolidate this reform and overcome of the dysfunctional forces embedded in the dynamic growth and massive changes that are occurring. A key area that local commentators are emphasising is that of an increasing need to take further steps to expand the scope of partnerships and strategic alliances between suppliers, carriers and service providers. This is to be expected given that network density has increased in many fields of technology and most recently especially in the fields of information technology and telecommunications.

Joint ventures among telecommunications

entities are becoming increasingly important, particularly as they relate to rising R&D costs. As telecommunications evolves in to a software-based industry, joint ventures grow in their attractiveness. Tunstall outlines how many consultants and scholars are expecting the telecom-computer industry to be dominated by giant consolidations of local, long-distance, and computer firms. This will be achieved through joint ventures, acquisition, mergers, and importantly, strategic alliances. The view is of a 21st century industry structure dominated by several global companies and a diversity of smaller niche product and service providers.

The issue of technology transfer discussed above and the process itself has raised the importance and complexities of joint ventures. This has been added to by new challenges emerging from the fields of marketing and distribution. Moreover, they offer advantages over mergers and acquisitions. These can be cost advantages but also the capacity to use the expertise of intact successful management teams, ones often destroyed in other processes.

In a recent article, Cutler, assessing continuing industry development arrangements, argues that government needs to encourage strategic alliances between telecommunications carriers and manufacturers, rather than manipulate domestic procurement policies. This builds on the strong interest in competition by collaboration and strategic alliances between carriers and suppliers, perceived generally as mandatory in the current environment. Such alliances, however, will result in major rationalisation within the industry. For some key firms with substantial infrastructure, employment and investment in Australia, there is a risk of significant disinvestment and employment effects with national implications. These alliances need to be far more than price based to achieve long term benefits.

The scale of these effects requires improvements in communication processes centring on close consultation with government and even government involvement to ensure that the eventual dislocation is both strategic and managed. This is clear given the very fundamental modification to industry processes that such alliances engender. The current revision of Telecom's relationships with suppliers gives clear indications of such changes. Ideally these new forms of alliances should include not only the carriers and large suppliers but also national interests reflected by government and the interests of the Small and Medium Enterprises. For the SMEs, steps should be taken to ensure that their interests are not overlooked. Proactive policy seems necessary to ensure that this sector is provided with an environment to grow. Strategic alliances are important to the SMEs because they could be used to support R&D, bridge capital and development shortfalls, spread risk, assist with market access both domestic and international, lift firms from sub-contractors to suppliers, and facilitate world best practice.

It also seems an opportune time to continue current and perhaps even introduce new mechanisms which foster the growth of companies among the Australian telecommunications SMEs into larger entities if that is considered appropriate. Alternatively, they might retain their present size but with increased robustness if that is seen as a more flexible and suitable design for the industry into the next decades.

The Partnerships For Development and Fixed Term Arrangement programs developed by the Commonwealth Government under the auspices of the Department of Industry, Trade and Regional Development, formerly provide a framework within which international and Australian companies can capture the international market opportunities in the information and communications industries. The focus of these programs is to enable companies and organizations to work together in developing new products and services within Australia and to win local, regional and new international markets.

In recognition of the fact that the information and communications industries are dominated by the mega international companies, both in Australia and internationally, these schemes encourage international companies to both strengthen and extend their Australian operations. Further, by using the resources of local firms and institutions, they can create new opportunities for a variety of stakeholders. The dynamic development of the Asia/Pacific region has, clearly, been a dominant concern here both for the international players and for Australia whose exports in the sector have grown from $650 million in 1987 to $1.5 billion in 1991 and which are expected to exceed $3 billion by 1995.

PFD programs are most suitable for those international companies with scale to government of over $40 million annually and FTA for those selling between $10 million and $40 million. Once a partnership is entered into with the Australian, State or Territory Governments an international company commits to reach and sustain a specified level of R&D and exports over a time frame agreed by the partners. Business plans and memoranda of understanding are part of the formal arrangements and the formation of strategic alliances with local organizations, mindful of what is commercially appropriate and viable, is strongly encouraged. Australian organizations become alliance partners through providing commercially useful products, skills and services to the international companies. Annual reviews of R&D, exports, strategic investments and import activities occur for companies involved in the schemes and the PFD program is audited by Ernst & Young.

Already about 300 Australian organizations are benefiting from these schemes particularly in terms of research and development and export strategies, Hypertec Pty Ltd, Australian Electronic Manufacturing Services, General Power Controls, ASPECT Computing, CSP software, LSE manufacturing etc.. Key among the many leading international companies that have participated in the programs are the following: Acer, Alcatel, Amdahl, Apple, BullHN, Canon, Compaq Computer, Concom, DEC, Ericsson, Fuji Xerox, Fujisu, GPT, Hewlett-Packard, Hitachi Data Systems, IBM, Ingres, Microsoft, NCR, NEC, Nokia, NorTel, Oki Electric, Oracle, Pyramid, Siemens Nixdorf, Storage Technology, Sun Microsystems, Tandem, Toshiba, Unisys and Wang.

As with the aerospace industry, Australian universities are also benefiting under these arrangements. For example, the US based Amdahl corporation has joint projects with La Trobe University in Melbourne, with Curtin University of Technology in Perth, and the University of Wollongong, through its Communications Technology Research Centre. So these programs do provide one option for the sort of strategic alliances that the sector wishes to develop. Though assessed by government and audited in financial terms and the like, little work has been done on the local/international alliance aspects of the program in terms of the issues we have covered earlier in this paper - intercultural communication and technology transfer.

Of more critical import is the current reassessment of Telecom's strategic equipment procurement policy with will have a major impact on many local Telecom suppliers in the electronics industry. Of particular interest is Telecom's equipment contract for switching and transmission systems, previously heavily the domain of Ericsson and Alcatel. American based organizations such as Nortel and AT&T are looming on the horizon. The organization is exploring its traditional relationships in the industry because of the competitive environment, particularly that of the new carrier, Optus and the more recent entrant, Vodafone.

The second Australian carrier, Optus, is a conglomerate, being owned by six major shareholders - four Australian and two overseas corporations. Moreover, from the beginning it has been based on strategic supplier relationships. It formed such agreements with six major companies, outlined initially in its Deeds with the Australian government, fostering industry development through research and development, technology transfer, export enhancement and the like. These strategic relationships are with Digital Equipment Corporation; Nortel Australia; Fujitsu Australia; Nokia Telecommunications; Olex Cables; and Leighton Contractors. The intercultural dimensions of these alliances are stunning. Yet, it is still early days for the real roll out of these relationships to be clearly defined as successful or not in any enduring sense.

One recent example of such relationships in the Australian telecommunications industry is that of the alliance between the global firm NorTel and Exicom, the latter Australia's largest listed company specialising in telecommunications. These two companies announced, on the 11th August 1993, a major new export initiative centring on the awarding of a five-year contract to Exicom to design, develop and manufacture a range of proprietary phones for NorTel to market to customers in Canada and the United States. Further, Nortel has appointed Exicom its global design centre for this new range of telephones catering for its North American customers. According to the Chief Executive Officer of Exicom the Exicom-NorTel strategic alliance has facilitated technology transfer via sourcing programs with NorTel and by a growing export business based on leading-edge technologies and design innovation. It was also reported that Exicom expected to increase production and services as a result of this alliance by $A45 million in 1994.

In spite of such recent success stories, underlying problems remain. For example, it is clear that there is an enormous amount of cultural similarity among the US, Canada, Australia and the UK. Yet, while similar, they are not identical as the research literature demonstrates. Even less similar are the cultures of the region in which we place so much faith for the telecommunications industry. Furthermore, Robert posits the view that many strategic alliances are likely to fail because they are formed for the wrong reason such as to correct a weakness. He advocates forming alliances to exploit unique strengths and alliances in which neither organization has the ability or desire to acquire the other's unique strength. Moreover, he argues that alliances often reduce competition, produce higher prices for the consumer, or breed complacency in the organizations involved. Tom Peters also warns against the return of bureaucratisation through badly managed alliances.

Clearly, strategic alliances should not be regarded as the latest fad in the quick-fix-it management tool kit. Conflicting interests, cultures and goals can undermine the very foundations of such business coöperation. Lewis argues that unless alliance partners have the same direction, have agreed on measures for success, and understand the need for mutual objectives, complementary needs, and shared risk taking, there will inevitably be problems. In alliances he emphasises that trust is pivotal, and is built on responsibility, equality, and reliability. Partners need to be chosen on combined commitment, strength, compatibility, and shared strategic objectives. Furthermore, evidence suggests that maintaining a balance between partners can be more difficult than determining precisely what that balance might be at the commencement of the alliance venture.

Further difficulties arise from the concern over losing competitive strength through the sharing of technology and, as Gugler argues, the real problems arise from organizational and national cultural misunderstandings and poor communication, as outlined earlier. Consequently it still appears uncertain what effect the emphasis of development of partnerships will have on the industry, on the future of technology, on consumers, government policy, and on the organizations involved.

Appendix

Transforming corporate culture in telecommunications industry

This article analyzes corporate culture transformation programs in the telecommunications industry. Specifically, it looks at (1) why a massive investment in corporate culture transformation has been deemed necessary, (2) ways it has been implemented, and (3) what some effects have been. It also suggests what these programs portend for the international scene.

Recent analysis of corporate culture generally views corporate performance as depending critically on a company's internal organization and operations. Consequently, executives seeking marketplace success increasingly attend to the 'corporate culture' dimension. For telecom companies, this dimension appears significant, particularly at the national and international business level. This is because telecom corporations are trying to mold workers and strategies drawn from various localities and sectors into cohesive business units as part of a global alliance strategy. But despite millions invested in altering corporate culture in US telecom companies, little systematic knowledge seems to exist about the relationship between this investment and claimed beneficial outcomes. Such knowledge should be relevant to American executives and scholars. It should also be relevant to international audiences as well since, just as the US has been on the forefront of liberalizing it telecommunications regulations, it has also been a leader in experimenting with new ways of marshalling human resources. Plus, US companies often act as bellwethers for non-American companies about potential options and risks.

Briefly, corporate culture means the social and symbolic system group members use as they work together to deal with their environmental situation. This system is relatively stable and persistent, encompassing beliefs, myths, symbols, patterns of behaviour, work practices, techniques, and structures of interpretation. It also encompasses informal and formal hierarchies. There is nothing superficial about corporate culture, contrary to what is implied in popular accounts. Rather, it constitutes a practical guide to action and an outlook by which people make their way, economically and socially, in the workplace. Finally, it is neither readily discardable nor divisible, but rather dynamic and adaptive.

Why telecom companies have sought to change their corporate culture

US telecom corporations are changing so they can succeed as their markets liberalize, customers become choosier, and ferocious competitors close in. Deregulation combined with rapid technological advances pose novel problems for telecom managers seeking to lead their organizations from its old environment to a new one. Reductions of staff, the magnitude of which is reflected in chart, also mean grappling with morale and continuity problems. For reasons explored next, managers often turn to corporate culture change programs as a crucial tool in these endeavors.

Unresponsive organization when environment demands fast change

Dramatic change in the telecom industry's environment has been a prime mover of corporate transformation programs. This change is especially striking in light of two factors. First, there previously had been in place a deeply embedded social order, the Bell culture. This culture was exceedingly strong, having evolved over more than a half century of highly stable regulatory regimes requiring only minor adjustments. This culture, successful for its time, was buffeted in the 1990s by novel forces. Second, since the industry's technology and manpower base had been stable, employees could exchange personal dedication for job security. In sum, the culture was fit for its time, but time have changed.

Another point about change in the telecom industry is that it takes only a handful of people acting in concert to drastically alter the industry's structure and composition. The daily activities for the half-million people who make up the telecom industry's workforce cannot change as fast. Their activities and beliefs will change only as fast as revise methods of operation are consistently adopted, percolate through the organizational ranks, and become absorb into daily routines. While a corporate shell is structured by the few, corporate culture is structured by the many.

As the telecom environment began rapidly

changing after 1983, some high-level corporate managers made an unsettling observation. After having given commands laying down new objectives or procedures, managers were often startled to find these were not being carried out. This unresponsiveness was a vexatious surprise since, under the old system, orders had been routinely executed. But under the new regime, even when instructions were carried out, they were often done so phlegmatically or only in letter, not spirit. To illustrate, one top telecom executive set annual performance review categories specifying that a minimum percentage of the workforce be classified in less desirable categories, and a maximum percentage in more desirable ones. Though these standard were met technically, employees were told by their immediate supervisors they were 'really' in a higher category, and their going along to appease the top executive would be appreciated. Obviously, the executive's wishes were not being carried out, and, when he discovered what was happening, became quite miffed and ordered the practice stopped.

During the 1980s, partially catalyzed by management consultants, consensus emerged among top telecom leaders that the reason for this decoupling of instruction from meaningful response was an ambient corporate culture inappropriate to the situation. Not the contrariness of individuals that inhibited the carrying out of orders, it was thought, but rather the culture itself.

Cultural transformation concept grew out of an evolving management theory tradition

Through 'corporate culture' as currently used blends several behavioral perspectives and strands of management theory, its key insight is an analytical framing of the workplace's socially constructed nature. Customs, legends, norms, vocabulary, attitudes, and beliefs are artifacts of an industry's organizational structure and history. The nature of this world affects the organization of production and the quality and speed of work. It suggests that culture is arbitrary, and therefore directly changeable and manipulateable.

In the past, this world, to the extent it was considered at all, was often viewed by management experts as either not important of sufficiently malleable. Taylor's 'scientific management' school did not care what workers believed or what their culture was so long as they carried out instructions. The human relations school was also uninterested in directly manipulating culture as a symbolic object, believing instead that with good, caring leadership, people would perform well; culture was not a concern as it would in effect take care of itself. Culture, or group dynamics as it was conceived of in the 1930s and 1950s was sometimes recognized by researchers, but often treated as an 'irrational' force requiring manipulation to fulfil management objectives. This has changed and corporate culture is now treated as a social reality worthy of study and engineering in its own right.

Concept is functional in light of decreased cultural homogeneity of entrants to management cadres

Organizational control hasdso been facilitated by the homogeneous nature of upper management levels, including spouses. Some aspects of the job were self-executing by virtue of shared values. However, a series of civil rights laws and court decisions beginning in the 1960s moved major companies to recruit in large numbers members of groups that had previously been under-represented or non-existent among the management ranks.

Before the civil rights laws, reasonably accurate assumptions about the nature and types of upper level telco employe were possible. Leaders and managers generally were white males fully involved in a lifestyle that included a specific form of self-presentation, both at and outside of work. Basic values were not only agreed upon but went unquestioned. Throughout the day, there was a shared, fully subscribed culture dictating specific norms, behavior, and jargon. The homogeneous national culture of the post-World War II American middle class was a build-in selection mechanism for new members of the corporate culture. The manners and outlooks of the middle-class male engineers and the dominant work ethos meant corporations could count on an 'installed base' of cultural lore. Official attention was rarely paid explicitly to the corporate culture of higher-level employees and managers.

With the influx of new employees - especially at managerial levels - not socialized to this culture, leaders had to find alternative ways of dealing with these new entrants. They needed to induct culturally diverse people into a dominant corporate culture. While great respect has been evinced for the relevant newly recruited sub-cultures, some might assert official respect and attention devoted to cultural diversity was really aimed at co-opting new entrants into the corporation's culture while minimizing the risk of discrimination lawsuits.

It was but a short step from the utility of giving an explicit 'cultural orientation' to new employees to intervening in the base culture itself. Doing so, it might be reasoned, would not only speed integration of new workers and managers, but also help regain cultural homeostasis.

Corporate belief structures often based on extra-rational criteria

Fashion also plays a role in what to emphasize. In the 1960s, the conglomerate style of business activity was the mode and such corporations as Litton, Allied-Signal, and Grace arose. It would not be uncommon for these corporations to combine disparate operations such as food sauce bottling, missile guidance system research, and car tire manufacturing all under one management umbrella. This approach is now out of style. Instead corporations are 'returning to basic strengths', reducing lines of business to a few central themes. We can ask if there is something inherently different about the business world in the 1990s than in the 1960s, and whether today's strategic planners are able to see things which escaped their predecessors. Addressing these questions is beyond our scope but the fact we can raise them suggests we should not minimize fashion and Zeitgeist when seekinr to understand corporate decision-making and behaviour.

What corporate culture transformation tries to accomplish

At a metaphysical level, an encompassing culture transformation seeks to replace the ailing life-blood of a corporation with a new vital blood. But despite the diversity of business enterprises and their environments in the US, there has been remarkable convergence of approaches: quality and customer focus are the shibboleths. The goal becomes how to transform the work environment and processes, the workers, and the image outsiders have of the company.

Work environment: build teamwork, accountability, and empowerment

The diagnosis of he corporate culture problem seems consistent across companies, and generally follows Deming's quality model, namely there has been a failure to (1) systematically address problems as well as (2) put the customer at the center of the organizational mission.

The first failure stems from top management's inability to grasp that major problems are almost always multifaceted. So even if well-motivated at the individual and corporate levels, there are structural impediments which if addressed in isolation cannot alone solve the problem. What is required is a total system, a holistic approach.

The second failure, related to the first, is that

internal operations and politics assume more importance than corporate mission. Cultural change advocates even go further to argue work-life in corporations is often structured to actually prevent individuals from contributing optimally, even if they so wish. When good performers have to struggle against a frustrating system, they become worn down and defeated. When sub-unit goals become more important than the total success of a corporation, the entire enterprise is hurt. When form rather than substance becomes preeminent, achievement suffers. Hence the goal of serving the customer can become supplanted by merely satisfying internal organizational requirements.

A solution suggests itself at an abstract level: require workers to operate in interdependent teams, evaluating them according to their contribution to group, not individual, goals. Team members need maximum discretion to make decisions, since they are most familiar with immediate exigencies and can readily alter directions. But to prevent excessive in-group stability from diminishing effectiveness, individual and group performance requires constant supervisory scrutiny, measurement, and stringent feedback to achieve ever-rising goals. The abstract level, though, is often hard to translate into daily operational regimes.

The worker: Intergrating all facet to focus on corporate problems

Corporate culture programs also seek to transform the individual in outlook and behaviour. But given that employees have many interests and commitments outside of the job, corporate leverage is limited. This makes it difficult to reach directly the individual's psyche. So these programs may try instead to draw on other aspects of society's values, beyond the corporation itself. But doing so can create strains concerning loyalty and personal goals. As Polanyi and others have noted, Western society is built on an economic system where production aims at profits, not social responsibility. Work is brutally competitive because market mechanisms are the central force. Work-life becomes organized not by intrinsic rewards but by extrinsic ones because in a market system price determines value, and people are forced to judge their worth by their income. This culture of instrumental and expressive individualism, some like Bellah argue, has become self-destructive. Yet it reflects the material reality in which we live, the logical working out of the market mentality. Despite this contradiction, corporate culture transformation seeks to integrate within the individual two antithetical values: materialism and transcendentalism. Ironically, by demanding ever-higher levels of commitment from workers, mainly by drawing on transcendental resources themselves become diminished and less available to be called upon in the future.

As a result, a contradiction arises in many corporate culture programs. The programs try to get employees to take individual responsibility and become active initiators rather than passive respondents. However employees are sometimes cajoled in ways which themselves militate against stated objectives. So for example, managers order employees to embrace the idea of group participation and democratic decision-making, but this goal and its desirability were secretly arrived at by a closed cadre of managers without inputs from the employees who putatively would be able to choose what they want. Managers and trainers want employees to drop barriers open communication channels, and not be afraid to engage in unconstrained thinking and inquiry. Buut the workshops designed to encourage this are run on strict time tables and employees are not allowed to question validity of constructs to be absorbed. Likewise there are sharp limits to initiatives and unconstrained thinking; off-limits for instance are questions about the sizes of particular managers salaries.

External environment: Alter perception of key audiences

The above aims are ultimately part of a strategy to improve the company's position relative to the external environment. The cultural changes implemented inside are directed towards influencing perceptions of those on the outside who affect the company's destiny. These outside include not just buyers of goods and services but also regulators and the general public. The term's ambit also includes possible competitors. Relative to each group, the culture change program lays another plate of armor to protect and enhance the company's position. Good corporate cultural change programs evaluate all aspects of the company's endeavor and consider carefully how to create a culture which will project to service and goods buyers the idea they will be optimally served by the telecom in question. Also considered will be ways to positively affect the perception of the telecom by regulators and the public. These steps will also help ward off potential competitors who might otherwise wish to invade the telecom company's markets. Thus a corporate culture not only structures the attitudes and behavior with an organization, but can also serve as an important strategic market advantage.

Program implementation: Issue and processes

Grand ideas about corporate culture change must be translated into specific programs. We look next at procedures often used to attain cultural transformation in US telecom companies.

Modalities for introducing a new culture

Telecom company culture transformations generally are undertaken using one or both of two approaches. The first is to introduce an outsider at the pinnacle of the company with a brief to change procedures. This happened at IBM, as well as British Telecom and Royal PTT Nederland. In all three companies, an outsider with market savvy or experience was brought in to help transplant a new culture. The 'change at the top' option can swiftly alter corporate culture. As part of this top level change approach, directorial boards, in contrast to their historical practice, increasingly rely on outside consultants for guidance. A second, more common approach is to bring in outside thinking without bringing in new top executives.

Instead, consultants are used to infuse the corporation with new thinking at the internal procedural level.

The corporate culture transformation process itself generally has three elements: re-engineering process synthetically creating teams, and re-socializing individuals to new goals, values and behaviors. The method of implementation entails some mix of sponsoring-corporation design with inputs from consultants. Consultants often believe they can have maximum impact if their program offerings and services are most widely embraced by their clients.

At one extreme we have the case of a US telecom company adopting the thorough-going recommendations of its consultants. It gave consultants a free hand to involve themselves in the company as they saw fit, all in the name of corporate culture transformation. This did not always sit well with employee who found their lives dissected by outsiders, especially when these outsiders saw it as their mission to change the direction and content of those lives. The process culminated in a series of intense indoctrination sessions in which employees had to vocalize certain beliefs and would be chastised if they did not sound sincere enough. At this juncture, relations between employees and consultants became so exacerbated that management had to pull-back sharply on the program.

More typical is for management to work intimately with consultants to formulate a series of workshops for employees. While the consultants stage-manage nearly everything, including training and overseeing workshop leaders, the company's top management remains central to the action and prominent in company-wide pronouncements. Ideas about cultural change are formulate by the consultants and refined via a committed of corporate representatives. After the high-level committees have passed on the recommendations, the corporate culture transformation machinery begins rolling. A collaboratively produced vision, style, and process, are enunciated by the company president, and a flurry of meetings and workshops follows.

A third style is to re-engineer via corporate resources with limited assistance from consultants. Re-engineering has been chosen by at least two US telecom companies. The way it has worked out, at least initially, is that numerous committees were organized under an umbrella re-engineering group. Several different corporate culture consultants were called in to provide pointers and review internally generated plans. All major systems and corporate process methods were analyzed with an eye to seeing if they were necessary, and if so, what extent they could be provided by outside sources at reduced cost. In many cases, a surprising range of activities are found to be unnecessary and so eliminated.

One example is a telecom company which had a home economics department. The department's purpose, contrary to what one might believe, was not to study economic aspects of the residential phone market. Rather it was to provide the telco's employees with information about sewing, house cleaning, and family meal menu tips. In an era of down-sizing and cost-containment, such popular but unprofitable operations are likely to disappear.

Sometimes re-engineering's impulse to raise efficiency can lead to radically divergent results. One telecom company began a 'charge-back' system where each staff unit would provide its services only if it would be 'paid' out of the requester's departmental budget. These were 'paper' transactions, but the purpose was to make everyone cost-sensitive and profit-motivated. It succeeded in this regard, but also reduced inter-departmental cooperation. Another collateral impact was that each department sought to duplicate in miniature the service capabilities of other service units within its own department.

Another company, though inspired by the same motive of cutting costs, took another path. It dropped a charge-back system as too costly and services that had formerly been levied against internal clients on a usage-sensitive basis were now provided at no cost. Any inefficiencies created by making the resources freely available were considered less than the costs of cumbersome tracking and accounting procedures. In addition, since a major component of the adopted reforms was 'empowerment', the workers would now be held accountable for their individual performance and expected to use corporate resources wisely, so central services would not be abused. Another result of this efficiency drive was to move purchasing and signature authority approval down one level of the hierarchy.

Though more people now had the capability to spend more money, empowerment presumably mean it would be less costly and speedier to get the goods and services needed. Overall costs should be less and operations sleeker. Employees felt more powerful and effective, and any unnecessary spending taking place was more than compensated by the decreased bureaucracy and associated costs required to authorize any spending.

Re-engineering can also empower customers. In one case, a company's division decided to eliminate any charge on a customer's bill that the customer claimed was incorrect. Previously the customer had to prove, or there had to be an independent confirmation, that the charge was invalid before it would be eliminated. But the company found that it not only usually cost more to adjudicate the bill than the amount in question, but that customers were upset by the process. The re-engineering proved to increase customer satisfaction and decrease cost. And it created more customer loyalty. By traditional accountability standards, this policy change would be a mistake, but from the view of customer-focused culture, it was the right choice.

Companies infrequently look for expert opinion from within their ranks, although given my definition of corporate culture this would be an important resource in any cultural adjustment attempt. Even when employee input is sought, it is often done through focus groups, which are problematical from the viewpoints of which employees are chosen to participate, how these individuals choose to participate, how the moderation is performed, and the manner in which the qualitative data is interpreted. A reason for not drawing on employees themselves to frame a program may be that corporate leadership does not believe it has people within the organization who could give the necessary guidance about corporate culture. This inclination is compounded by the hierarchical nature of large telecom companies. Plus, legitimate concerns exist that insiders would bias any recommendations. There are additional tactical reasons for utilizing consultants. As an example, their imprimatur might carry more weight, or they can be bearers of information best not be seen as coming from people or units within the corporation. Consultants could bear responsibility for unpopular ideas without having to remain on site to deal with the aftermath, deflecting anger from the executive whose will they actually were carrying out. This was the case when a company changed its logo; it was an inside move attributed to outside consultants who essentially endorsed what management said they wanted, leaving management blameless.

Fragile barrier between private/public, individual/corporation, psychological/operational

Change can be traumatic. Recognizing this, most corporate culture programs have a module to help employees deal with stress. Included are topics such as behavioral and philosophical advice, breathing and positive visualization exercises, stress management techniques. They also subsume methods which allow employees to deal more effectively with others, not just co-workers but customers, service personnel, and family members as well. A key goal is to help employees set and pursue personal objectives, as well as persuade them to adopt certain beliefs about self-realization and self-direction.

It was precisely these initiatives which led fundamentalist Christian employees to criticize one telecom company because its change program, they felt, was trying to force them to adopt values which conflicted with their religious views. Corporation-engendered beliefs such as 'you can make it happen', or 'you control your own destiny' flew in the face of these employees' beliefs that only God decides what happens in one's life, and that He controls one's destiny. These criticisms of the corporate culture program were taken so seriously that an extremely extensive initiative had to be terminated.

Corporate culture transformations themselves can also have a paradoxical impact on employees. This is because, on the one hand, they can empower employees. Workers have greater authority to make decisions and try innovations. But in another way their freedom decreases: detailed benchmaking and minutely specified performance goals are set-down and the measures of success and the consequences of failure are unambiguous and inescapable. Moreover, more employees become monitored more frequently.

Here I am not talking about blue or pink collar workers, such as installers and operators who traditionally have been held to detailed, exacting, and real-time performance standards. Instead I am referring to sales, marketing, software operations personnel, and other white collar and middle management who traditionally are evaluated at the end of a month, or even at the end of a year, and then sometimes by rather arbitrary, qualitative indicators. After the corporate culture transformation, these people are often measured and 'benchmarked' weekly or, in the case of some cellular service sales people, even hourly. So in this sense their freedom and autonomy has been reduced, and the feedback loop has been tightened considerably. A by-product then of corporate culture change can be the bringing under the management microscope levels of employees who had heretofore been exempt.

New vocabularies for a new nomic order

Companies can purchase various degrees of corporate culture transformation from consultants. Often there is an emphasis on packaged modules. Naturally, the greatest effects are promised only in those cases where all modules are purchased. But as indicated, this ;can require a substantial organizational commitment, often to an untested method. As is characteristic of most corporate education and training operations, the emphasis is on containerization, portability, attractive packaging, and 'workshop' methods.

In the workshops themselves, central themes revolve around personal empowerment and accountability, teamwork, priority-setting, responding to customer needs, and quality. Part of the re-socialization process is accomplished with new phrases and jargon. Hence, instead of saying 'we agree', the phrasing may now be 'we have come into alignment on the path forward'. The reasoning for this phrasing is that 'agreement' is static, 'path forward' and 'alignment' are dynamic. Further, by being required to use new terminology, workers are forced to become consciously aware of the new values and culture.

The vocabulary can also have hortatory and inspirational uses. One large telecom company, code-named here as 'Newtel', had on its annual report cover the statement, 'The watchwords of the Newtel Way are 'teamwork','accountability', and 'empowerment', the characteristics we believe will be the key to success in a global marketplace'. Inside, were quotes from employees, one of whom said:

> I think the Newtel Way energizes our people. It encourages them to take control over their jobs, to be creative to take risks, and to manage their own careers.

These statements reflect Newtel's serious commitment to the program and its adoption throughout the company. Interestingly, in a recent visit to Newtel headquarters executive suite, I saw that the corporate art had been replaced with large, boldtext posters containing key phrases from the workshops.

Below the symbolic level lies the more prosaic one of fluent intra-organizational communication, which a shared vocabulary can yield. By having agreed-upon phrases and meanings, it is easier to get messages clearly across to others, a virtue most readily appreciated in a heterogeneous environment where dispatch is a virtue. The military, aware of this for millennia, has made sciences of standardizing instructions and word-meanings.

So, on the one hand, an individual employee might use a phrase learned in the workshop to quickly get her meaning across. For example, employees might have been taught in the workshop that an urgent, vital project is a 'blue chip'. Hence such a term can be a tool to let others know one's evaluation of a project's priority. We find such a use cited in Newtel's annual report, which quoted a senior buyer in purchasing as saying:

> When all you have to do is say 'blue chip' and people know that means top priority, it helps you communicate more effectively, it helps you get more done.

An unintended consequence of these new vocabularies, on the other hand, is that they can become, as Clausewitz said of war, politics carried on by other means. A core purpose to terms like 'blue chip' is to signal others that the 'blue chip' project must be placed above individual or departmental priorities. But a distinction between a real corporate priority and a strictly departmental advantage can often be elusive. The temptation exists, unconsciously or not, for people to use it to advantage. Advocates of a project can misuse workshop vocabulary to persuade others to do what the advocates wanted anyway, only more easily. Something valuable for one business unit may, in an advocate's mind, qualify as a 'blue chip for the corporation', increasing the legitimacy of the unit's demands on corporate attention and resources while simultaneously neutralizing opponents. Nonpriority programs may receive new window dressing to fit within key corporate rubrics and may even gain extra momentum. If one disagrees with a blue chip designation, that individual becomes liable to being accused of bridling the new cultural regime, or at least of being insufficiently indoctrinated. In essence, while principles can be designed to help a corporation, careless implementation boomerangs.

For the time being

Time, among other things, is a key variable in corporate culture interventions. A core concept is the notion that time is a resource to be managed and exploited. There is a cottage industry in the US of time-management workshops, time-management technologies, and detailed time accounting. It is no accident 'time-motion' studies originated in the US.

Specifically in this context is the view of time

as a corporate resource which must be put to service. An old chestnut is that time is one thing that cannot be created, and that everyone has the same twentyfour hours in a day. However, many of the corporate culture techniques are designed to create more time.

This is done of course not physically but mentally. Techniques are taught to save time and to work with more efficiency and concentration. Priority-setting is taught, with an emphasis on dropping low-value projects and activities so more time will be available for high pay-off ones. Techniques are also presented about how to conduct efficient meetings. Within the priority framework, workers are enjoined that killing time is not murder, but suicide. Time is to be conserved and dedicated to purposeful action every bit as much as corporate purchases, or use of electrical energy or petrol. These efforts can actually 'create' more time which can be productively applied to corporate ends.

Responses of employees and the indigenous culture

Employees greet attempts at cultural transformation in numerous ways, predicated largely on their personal experiences, and their perceptions of the company and its external environment. However the manner in which the transformation program itself is undertaken also influences employee responses.

This can be seen in one instance when a jargon phrase incorporated in a training session was 'time-thieves'. To illustrate the concept of numerous small activities and inadvertent occurrences that waste time, the consultants displayed cartoons depicting small gremlins carrying bags on their backs dubbed 'time', stealing away from the corporate offices. Shortly after the training session, an anonymous group within the company began circulating their own literature encouraging employees to work against the corporate culture program by becoming 'time thieves' - waste the company's time, be as unproductive as possible, they were urged.

So resistance to change can take many forms; resisters can turn the new culture symbols against those in power. In another instance a telecom company installed at key locations colorful bulletin boards labeled 'culture transformation station'. Their purpose was to update employees about the company's new culture as it was enduring a 'down-sizing'. In a professional wing, someone plastered the bulletin board with application forms for entry level jobs as 'burger-flippers' at McDonald's. The prank was enjoyed sardonically by employees for a few hours until top management noticed the postings and quickly removed them. But presumably these guerrilla actions do not delay the program's onslaught.

Employee reactions often fall into one of four categories. The first reaction is that here is an important new way of doing business and increasing personal effectiveness. Employees of this ilk might think they will need these new skills if they are to perform and excel in their jobs. They immediately embrace the words and concepts, using them in their daily experience. It may be that among these enthusiastic employees there are some who have private reservations about the program. But if so, there is nothing in their presentation-of-self to reflect any doubt or hesitation. They behave perfectly, evincing no action, gesture, or eye-rolling to suggest they are not in full agreement with what is happening.

A second group also tries to understand and use the system. But rather than becoming 'converts' or enthusiastic proselytic proselytizers, these people openly express their doubts, hesitations, and difficulties in understanding and adopting corporate culture schemes. At the same time, they are willing to put forth the effort necessary to comply with the new cultural norms. They might be considered good but uninspired employees, and probably represent the largest segment of workers.

A third group is simply unenthusiastic. They approach the corporate culture operation as just one of an endless series of attempts to improve organizational performance. They will do the minimum necessary to stay out of trouble and give exceedingly modest endorsement when called upon. Mostly, though, they sit quietly and politely during the program, but express their dissatisfaction sub rosa during the breaks.

A final group will actively challenge the program. They will ask difficult, diverting, and problematical questions of the workshop moderators. They will try to find logical or operational flaws in the program. If provoked enough, the implementers of the transformation program will react. The moderator's first response may well be to use various co-optation techniques, such as soothing he question-poser, agreeing that something might be true about the assertion, or expressing gratitude for the contribution. Then the moderator will quickly try to move on. However, if the troublemaker persists, heavier sanctions will be imposed.

Changing focus from reception to content, what actually transpires at these meetings can be summarized as a combination of training session, revival meeting, and old-fashioned American boosterism. There is a moral undertone suggesting the new culture is superior to its predecessors, not only in its service of the company's interests, but also in its service to individual employees.

Yet when the new is praised, it may seem the old is being indicted. In the US telecom case, though, the old culture has in fact been celebrated for decades. One business magazine described 'the Bell culture' as having once been 'the company's most treasured asset'. This culture, though, is now accused of being insensitive to customer needs and unresponsive to its environment. Yet in my opinion, the Bell culture was highly responsive to customer needs, but in the old days the customer was different.

But workshops, posters, slogans, and lectures combined are still insufficient for an effective corporate culture change. Top managers themselves occupy a pivotal role in a successful transformation process. It may be the case that top management, though they advocate a new culture for the employees, do not change their own behavior -it is for others, but not themselves. This attitude was shown by one officer who complained bitterly at having to move from his penthouse suite in the corporate skyscraper - a location he had devoted his life to attaining - down to the third floor. This was required by the officer's CEO so the officer would demonstrate his support for the new culture.

Still, top managers' failure to 'walk the talk' can drastically reduce employee acceptance of corporate culture change programs. One consequence is employees will migrate from supporters to cynics. This is illustrated by one instance of an employee, inspired by the notion workers should be able to think independently and without fear of freely expressing themselves, put under his Email signature a quote from a famous person espousing free expression and discussion.6 After a while, senior management informed the individual:

> Your reference ... is cute, but getting a little old. Perhaps it is time to leave it off your Email.

Feeling a long shadow cast over him, the employee hastily deleted it. The cost to the company was to increase his cynicism about management's belief in the desirability of open expression and frank communication within the corporation.

This instance is important because it highlights misunderstandings that can arise when implementing corporate cultural transformations. It shows the futility of thinking that cultural transformation must be applied to employees but that the bosses are exempt. The attitude reflected borders on a view of employees as children who have to be manipulated. But people are not as easily duped as our models might have us believe; white collar workers seem reasonably adept at distinguishing sincerity from artifice. No members of an organization are above or outside its culture. A more realistic analogy might be people in a swimming pool: they are all in the same water together. This view stems from a broad definition of culture, namely that it represents a systematic adaptation of all members of the relevant group to each other and to their environment. It is unrealistic to expect that bosses could stay the same while employees are to change; acting as if this assumption were true will only lead to disenchantment. Finally it shows both in form and substance that when people are free to choose, those in power may not always like the choices which are made.

Significantly, corporate culture change really means bosses cannot have it both ways. Presumably the discomfort they experience by allowing employees the autonomy to make choices later deemed undesirable by bosses will be transient, while the benefits of greater employee efficacy will add to the boss' long-term gratification.

In sum, corporate culture transformation is not only an idea, but a commercial package and a social process. As such, style, timing, and procedure will affect its assimilation and effectiveness. Commitment and meaningful behavioral change emanating from the top appears critical to a successful program.

Meaning for international operations

In this section we explore the international implications of corporate culture transformation, first by referring specifically to the European context, then to the international scene as a whole, which of course also encompasses Europe. The industrialized/less-developed country dichotomy, useful in other contexts, has little relevance here since pre-existing infrastructure can be leap-frogged by new technologies. Telecom services available via technologies such as low-orbiting satellites, cellular systems, and digital networks offer coextensive plausibility for countries of otherwise widely varying levels of industrial development.

European scope

American corporate culture programs have implications for European telecoms, especially those desiring to work with the companies that were created by the Bell system's breakup. A primary concern, though, is whether a cultural transformation 'American-style' is even appropriate for European telecom companies. Perhaps the answer is less important than the reality that, given the American model's power in so many European areas of life, the desire to adopt such programs will be strong, regardless of their efficacy. Should American telecom companies which have been 'culturally transformed' begin pulling ahead of their more decorous counterparts, and especially if they meet with great success in Europe, such an attraction may well prove irresistible. This should be true even if the corporate culture transformation programs were irrelevant to the telecom company's success. So in this sense, any judgments as to corporate culture programs' perceived appropriateness, or even their actual appropriateness, could be irrelevant since they may be undertaken anyway.

Still, there are factors which could moderate if not arrest such a program, particularly in the thorough-going American form. The first of these is the strong European tradition and laws of protecting individuals in the workplace, protection to a degree unimaginable to most Americans. These laws might well hobble use of some aggressive methods of instilling a new culture among the workforce.

European telecoms often have a civil service tradition which has created a unique, deeply entrenched culture that must be confronted in any 'transformation'. For many European countries, there is also a strong labour union tradition which could impede such attempts. These factors, combined with the larger European ethos of human rights, will likely preclude the Draconian measures, such as surprise firings and immediate expulsions of surplus personnel from their offices, which has accompanied a few American corporate culture retooling programs.

At the same time, the European companies will need to either transit from norms and behaviors appropriate to monopolistic settings or else face extinction. The chosen method, though, is likely to be incremental, rather than the extreme steps characteristic of some American companies.

Certainly there will be no lack of consulting companies, both US and European, offering culture transformation services. But it will be difficult to know which companies are selling performance, and which are selling hype. Also there would be question whether past successes with other companies, to the extent they could be documented, were due to their contribution instead of some other party or even some unique circumstances. Finally there would be some question as to whether these skills are truly appropriate for the European telco considering their services. By the same token, as alluded above, the benefits of a fresh look by outsiders, or having an independent source of recommendations, should not be underestimated.

Further, the major European telcos attend carefully to what their colleagues in other EU nations are doing. They also imitate each other to a degree, moving gradually along more or less in tandem. Rather than a weakness or evidence of a lack of imagination, some major European telcos view it as advantageous to do things the same way as their counterparts in other countries. To give an example I share an anecdote from a participant at a top-level meeting where the national PTT of country D was considering what to call itself as it became a privatized entity. The PTT wanted a new image and was inclining towards calling itself 'D-Telecom', but its consultants wanted a more exiting, novel name, something like 'Ultra-Com'. At a meeting to decide on the name, the consultants presented charts showing among the 'good reasons' to change to a novel name was that three other European PTTs had already called themselves 'A-Telecom', 'B-Telecom', and 'C-Telecom', respectively. A novel name, they said, would help distinguish PTT-D from the competition. However, when the directors of PTT-D grasped what the other PTTs had done, insisted the point be moved from the column of 'good reason' to 'bad reasons' for a novel name.

On the other hand, with liberalization there will be many new entrants to the European market. New companies have the advantage of being able to create their corporate culture when they begin operations. Built-in resistance will be less, while rewards and behaviors can be immediately structured to address current market exigencies. they will not need to devote effort transitioning their workforce from its old ways, an expense the former PTTs would have to bear.

However, beyond the areas we have been discussing lie issues of the relative regional and national differences in corporate culture. As a telecom business expands its global organizational connections, its corporate culture becomes ever more critical, especially as it begins interacting with other distinctive regional cultures.

International scope

The historical pattern of separate nation-based telcos is becoming increasingly archaic. Future telecom player will be truly global entities, with adjustments to local employment practices made where necessary. Within this context, corporate culture objectives may become more directed toward integrating diverse practices and perspectives rather than on re-tooling a static, procedure-dominated organization into a dynamic customer-focused one. The complexities of fast-moving, specialized markets demand flexibility, and farflung operations require integration. These exigencies suggest a convergence on a style that incorporates multiple frames of reference and rapidly shifting skills.

International business strategy requires exploitation of foreign markets and working with members of the host culture. Global telecom company representatives clearly must be able to provide an interface between local cultural practices and the culture which operates within the telecom company.

We have crossed the threshold into an era of cross-national alliances. This effectively means bringing nationals of diverse cultures together in operations. Under these conditions the normal difficulties of communication are amplified. Without sensitivity to local cultural practices and incentives, one can easily founder. As Nomey

Wachtel pointed out, literal translation is not sufficient to understand what is going on in a host culture. She cited her experience where she and her AT&T colleagues went to a newly opened Eastern European nation to negotiate a telecom contract. Each side was constantly having to explain to the other its way of doing business. All of this time and effort was independent of the substance of the negotiation itself and occurred at all levels. Despite much effort, occasional farcical resulst could not be avoided. In a memorable incident, the American team failed to understand the crucial role of gift exchange with service providers, the consequence of which was that they were turned out of their hotel in favor of more generous gift-givers. From a cultural viewpoint. foreign entanglements are pregnant with possible conflicts and rewards, and, retrospectively, a source of amusing anecdotes.

As different cultures having a distinct regional or national identity are brought into integrated working relationships, the 'cultural baggage' of the larger societies will inevitably conflict within the more limited corporate culture boundary. The US has already had a foretaste: not surprisingly in such a vast, diverse country like the United States, there are vast differences in regional culture. How could, for instance, the important but widely varying local norms about racial minority hiring be adhered to by a national company like AT&T. In the 1950s and early 1960s, these sometimes strict local norms were often nearly the opposite in various state jurisdictions.

The practice is one state would be unacceptable to another, yet all these companies were under the same corporate umbrella.

Although this is an historical referent, corporate culture is important even in the contemporary scene when companies attempt to create domestic alliances or mergers. Hence, the 1994 fizzling of what was going to be the largest merger in American business history - between Bell Atlantic and Tele-Communications Inc. - has been attributed primarily to a conflict between cultures and philosophies.

On a different plane, but similar theme, I have been informed by Swedish employees of British Telecom that they discern a conflict between the hierarchical arrangements which are typical of BT and the more muted status distinctions typical of Swedish companies. Likewise, there may be some difficulties encountered in partnerships such as that between US WEST and France Telecom. There will be points of contact between those, on the one hand, who are steeped in the free spirit of cowboys and the unbridled freshness of the frontier with those, on the other hand, who are steeped in the tradition of Napoleon and beaux arts. Doubtless many of these interactions will produce valuable synergism and enriching experiences. It will also probably be the case that without adequate staff preparation, different cultural norms and practices will impede smooth communication and coordination.

With globalization of the telecom business, we can expect a rapidly shifting potpourri of corporate partnerships, strategic alliances, spun-off subsidiary operations, and acquired smaller companies in niche markets. This cacophonous admixture may make the corporation harder to manage; it will certainly make it less amenable to centralized control from the top. Perhaps having a shared core of values, vocabulary, and inter-oprable conceptual tools will allow the corporations to maximize the advantages of scale while minimizing the costs of ponderousness. Having a unified core culture, yet one still respecting local autonomy and initiative, may be a vital advantage. Such a culture would presumably respect diversity, combine individual autonomy and responsibility, plus - something difficult to achieve - reward risk-taking. It would be a culture where frames of reference can shift rapidly and empathetically, where conflicting ideas and interpretations can co-exist, and individual meaning and cultural identity will have an integrated, artfully constructed quality. Rather than gradual transitions characteristic of the past, the future telecommunications environment will have sharp discontinuities in meaning and method. A post-modern corporate culture, then, for a postmodern corporation.

Coda

Culture is demonstrably important in achieving both corporate performance objectives and effective cooperation with strategic partners. The old cultural forms of many telecom companies appear inappropriate to emerging business environments. Corporate leaders, frustrated by slow-reacting bureaucracies, find compelling the far-reaching transformation promised by corporate culture reconstruction. The key question, though, is whether the explicit 'cultural transformation' being practiced by some companies is apt. Such programs are expensive, both in direct costs and in time and emotional costs to employees. Many argue that gradual, calm approaches used by other companies are preferable. Unfortunately we do not have the direct evidence necessary to give a clear answer. But my personal observations do suggest that the manner in which these programs are implemented, regardless of their speed, makes a difference in their effectiveness.

There are experts who see quick action as best, instantly dispatching surplus employees. They say if the procedure is more deliberate, those who are going to be eliminated will poison other employees and be daily reminders of past problems and portents of future gloom. Supporters of this view hold that by eliminating surplus workers immediately, and shocking those remaining by 'lessons of the new environment', they are acting humanely. It allows all parties to make personal and professional adjustments in light of new realities. Dragging matters out is a disservice to those who either must now pursue other career options or reorient their daily routines within the corporation.

Different experts say this approach -rather than being more humane - is cruel. Advocates of a 'gradualist' approach say that by giving employees time to make adjustments, they are allowing them to maintain their dignity even while losing their jobs. The lesson given to the remaining employees is they are part of a benevolent company which takes care of its deserving people. The unstated reciprocal is the corporation in return deserves employees' respect and dedication.

Which alternative is preferable remains firmly lodged in the sphere of values since, so far as I have been able to determine, there has been no systematic evaluation that would allow us to definitively answer this question. Still, beyond the issues of internal company management, these personnel retention and acculturation decisions have ramifications for the larger business environment of these companies. Thus treatment of workers in a semi-regulated industry can be an object of interest for both governmental bodies and labour unions. It also has implications for the recruitment and retention of the most talented workers. And in some very rare cases, these decisions have become the concerns of very high levels of governmental political leadership.

Opinions abound as to what should be done, but little firm data exists. Yet the scattered evidence disposes me to conclude that several factors seem to increase the likelihood of the success of corporate culture programs.

First, top and middle management should evince a clear, sustained and meaningful dedication to the program. The sustained aspect is important. Little can make employees skeptical faster than the 'vital organizational objective du jour' syndrome. A dangerous gap can emerge between verbal commitment and behavioral follow through, as there can between initial and longrun commitment. And the bigger the gap, the less effective the program. Employees who have been through the workshop wringer will be rightly skeptical if managers simply mouth empty phrases. Further, the previous year's enthusiastic campaign cannot be quietly discarded since attentive employees have elephant memories.

Second, incentives should exist for employees to 'buy into' the new system. They need to see that it will work well and to their benefit, and it is better if these be demonstrated quickly. Employees must be persuaded that what they themselves understand and recognize align with management's prescription for change. For, as Robert K. Metron said, 'organizational decisions become transformed into organizational realities only to that extent that they engage the willing support of those who must translate them into day-by-day practice'. Also valuable is making a concerted effort not to degrade the prior culture.

Third, pacing is crucial albeit problematical. Chestger Barnard, a leading organizational analyst of the 1930s described it as the 'tune kag dukenna'. By this he meant the enduring friction between an organization's need for rapid adaptive action and the slow process through which its employees grasp the value of, and give their legitimacy to, the action. Unrelenting attention must be paid to lags in understanding to reduce friction and increase solidarity and effectiveness.

Fourth, and related to the above points, employees should be informed in a straightforward, honest and adult-like way what is going to be happening. They need to see that the company's approach is a reasonable, and reasoned, and that the entire enterprise has been thought through carefully. By shielding employees from the bad news, faith in the program and corporate leadership is sapped. Worse, it prevents employees from coming to mature understandings and acceptance of hardships and challenges. Trying to freighten them through exaggeration has similar bad consequences.

Fifth, the culture transformation program should emphasize the essentially humane concern of the company. It is not contradictory to do this even while firing people. Though some employees might not care what kind of company they work for, most seem to want to take pride in their organization, and know they are marking the world a better place for their efforts.

A strand underlying my remarks is that while opinions abound, hard data permitting us to create meaningful categories and assessments about approaches to changing cultures are not available. Perhaps a prudent next step would be a social mapping project. This project would attempt to delineate what points are important about the major corporate and indigenous cultures, what aspects of these cultures might lead inherently to conflict, and how these cultural values and processes relate to corporate and strategic alliance effectiveness.

A danger - which good data should help mitigate - is that proposed solutions frequently seem superficial and transient, or, as one anthropologist observed, 'the concept of corporate culture is too often a glib prescription rather than an expression of reality'. While management can take some fundamentally important actions about corporate culture, these actions must be predicated on a proper understanding of culture. Ironically, the concept is often not well defined in management/workshop literature, and to the extent it is defined, it is not a good a definition.

As argued at the outset, corporate culture is all of a piece, always changing, adapting. Hence the notion of an 'old culture' in need of eradication or replacement is faulty. So too is a program which expects employees to 'really change' their outlook and actions - their culture - but does not require the same of top executives. It is also a misjudgment to believe top executives can 'pick and choose' which parts of the culture are to be kept, which discarded. It is an integrated system serving a variety of implicit and explicit purposes and not simply a response to a command. People can often figure out improvements to operations if given a chance. But this chance seldom arises despite management's publicly swearing allegiance to 'empowerment'. In other words, culture is capable of responding and successfully adapting on its own, given authentic signals from both the external environment and the internal hierarchy.

The problem is not with the concept of changing culture but rather the method and narrow goals used. A distressing proportion of change programs take a superficial tack, applying a standardized gloss rather than addressing deeply the content of work. Ultimately, work is something people accept, and generally identify with. This acceptance can become a tremendous force if leveraged and worked with. But this requires detailed, specific knowledge of the existing corporate culture and its inherent mechanisms of change, not simply the ability to sell and administer a generic package.

The difficult task ahead is to understand the internal dynamics of corporate culture and its links to the larger external culture; only then can we know more precisely how to appropriately modify it.

Index